THE TRUTH ABOUT YOU

Timeless Truths About Finding Your

Purpose In Life

———————— By ————————
Peter Gabriel

THE TRUTH ABOUT YOU

Timeless Truths About Finding Your Purpose In Life

email: publishing@skylinemedia.tv

website: www.skylinemedia.tv

Unless otherwise indicated, all scripture quotations are from the New King James Version of the Bible.

Copyright 2010 by Peter Gabriel. All rights reserved

No part of this publication may be produced, distributed or transmitted in any form or by any means, including photocopying, recording or other electronic or mechanical methods, without the prior written permission of the publisher, except in the case of brief quotations embodied in critical reviews and certain other non-commercial uses permitted by copyright law. For permission requests, contact the publishers at the address above via post or email and make request addressed 'permission for copyright use'.

Photography by Photo Memories, Kent

Published by Life and Success Media

www.abookinsideyou.com

ISBN Number: 978-1-907402-84-5
Cover Design: miadesign.com

Dedication

I dedicated this book first and foremost to my Creator, for giving me the wisdom and knowledge to package these truths that he has put inside me and the experiences he has put me through. I also dedicate this book to my parents, most especially my mother for her constant prayers for me to reach my full potential and purpose. To my family, my three daughters, Zoe, Zara and Zandra, they have been a pillar of strength and support in my journey of the realisation of me. Finally, to my one and only, my backbone, the one that always has my back, that knows when to protect me from the outside world, my darling wife, Bisi

Acknowledgements

My Pastor, Dr Tayo Adeyemi, for his teaching, encouragement and care for his flock. Mr David Adabale and the whole Multimedia team of New Wine Church in London for their support, you are my family. To my spiritual father, Pastor Michael Olawore, for his continued support, guidance, encouragement, prayer and his belief in me. Thank you.

Table Of Contents

Dedication 3

Acknowledgements 5

Foreword . . . .

Introduction . . . .

Chapter

1. Your View 'Who Am I' 11

2. The Facts About You
   'Your Creator's View' 25

3. Your Attitude 'You Are
   Who You Say You Are' 39

4. Your Habits And Character
   'Your Make Up' 61

5. Your Values And Belief System
   'Who You Become' 89

6. Your Blueprint 'Your Roadmap
   To Your Destiny' 107

7. Your Purpose 'Your Reason
   For Being You' 143

8. Success 'Your Destination' 161

   Epilogue 177

   References 181

Preface

Finding your purpose in life is one of the most rewarding things that can happen to you. For some people, it can take a lifetime, for some the experience eludes them completely, and for others, it's as clear as day. But for me, finding and embracing my purpose happened before my fortieth birthday.

I was off work and decided to attend a free training course. I got on the train, said a little prayer, and then it hit me; I had longed for this moment, the feeling was that of fulfilment and completion. I felt exactly how you will feel when you find something that is of most value to you; I finally found the missing jewel in my crown.

Over my years of existence, I have come to the realisation that you need to find the definite purpose for your life, the reason why you were created.

James Allen, the 19th century British philosopher and poet, puts it like this, 'Your vision is the promise of what you shall one day be'. I say, 'Your vision is your key to your future'.

With a vision of your life, you can tap into unimaginable abilities that lay dormant inside you, waiting to be activated. Knowing your purpose enables you to know that you were not created to just pass through life unnoticed. Knowing your purpose tells you what you are suppose to contribute to your generation.

'The Truth About You' takes you on a journey of who you see yourself to be, who your creator see's you as, and a road map to getting to who you really are, and what you are called into the earth to fix. Every human being is an answer to a question, you just need to find the question. Business tycoon Warren Buffett said, and I quote, "Someone's sitting in the shade today because someone planted a tree a long time ago," that is vision. You have to find your calling and act on it.

This book will help you find the facts about you that you didn't know, rekindle the dreams inside you that you thought you could not achieve, and help you draw up a plan that will lead you to finding YOURSELF and YOUR position in the jigsaw of life. *The Truth About You* will help you overcome the obstacles that hinder you from being YOU.

Chapter 1

Your View 'Who Am I'

'You are who you say you are. You be who you say you be'

How You See Yourself

It has been said that, you make your own luck, well, that statement is true. In life, we wonder for years on our life treadmill, doing a lot of walking, but going nowhere. We wake up, go to work or college, we eat, we go to sleep, we wake up and start another day. Days become weeks and weeks become months and months become years and then we get old and look back and sometimes say, I could have or I should have, but didn't. We spend so much time in life being busy, living an unfulfilled life, when we have the ability to live a fulfilled and meaningful one.

However, we eventually die and everything good that the creator put inside us goes into the ground and there goes another question asked, not answered.

Ralph Waldo Emerson, the 19th century great philosopher said, and I quote;

"The purpose in life is not to be happy, it is to be useful, to be honourable, to be compassionate, to have it make some difference that you have lived and lived well."

It is very important to have an understanding of the reason for your existence. When we look at history, we talk about our forefathers, the forerunners before us, people that walked this earth and made their lives count for something. I thank God everyday for the sacrifices that were made so that I can be where I am today. If our past heroes had not answered the call, and deposited what was in them into this world, there would be none of the possibilities, nor the inventions that have made living comfortable and enjoyable in this time that we are living. Inventions such as the light bulb, the air conditioner, the mobile phone, the computer, game consoles and lots more. All these inventions came into existence because they decided that they would answer the questions that were asked; the reason they were born into this world. We are enjoying the labour of our heroes past and there is a demand on us to deliver to the next generation. We are to answer the questions that were asked for us to get the call to duty, the reason why we were born.

Who do YOU see yourself to be? Who do you think you are? At your funeral, what would be said about you? On your tombstone what will be written of you? These are questions you should ask yourself and should be able to answer whether good or bad. The author and self-achievement specialist, Napoleon Hill said;

'Ninety five percent of the vast majority of people go around and around without an aim or purpose, they drift with the circumstances of life, good or bad'.

Are you one of the ninety five percent or are you part of the five percent that are the successful individuals that are living a fulfilled life?

Psychology experts who have studied human behaviour and personality have classified people into different categories dependent on specific attributes they exhibit. The primary reason for these classifications is to fit individuals into boxes that allow them to manage each other relationally. I am not knocking personality check products, I even believe they can be useful depending on how you use them however, if all you do is place yourself in a personality box, you are limiting your mental capacity and personal ability. I believe, this is using the tool in a negative way; this is my opinion of course.

I recently returned to work after some time off and I was in conversation with some colleagues that just got back from holiday too. Everyone was telling stories of how they enjoyed their holidays and how they did not want it to end, but they all had one statement in common, 'now back to reality'.

Have you ever thought about enjoying your life all the time? Have you ever felt that there is more to your life than just waking up, going to work, coming home eating and going to sleep, going on holiday once or twice a year? I know I did for a very long time.

Personality

Society has defined you through psycho-analysis using charts, tests and questionnaires. This has become a major area in finding out what makes the human being tick. These personalities have even been characterised into types of temperaments, these different temperaments are being used to guide the way in which we see and judge each other according to our behaviours, actions, and attitudes.

These labels determine how the world classes individuals into boxes that tell you how you behave, what type of work you can do, who you can relate with and who you can not relate with. These personality boxes are actually true when you accept the construction of your mindset from birth growing into adulthood, however, the real truth is, 'IT IS WHO YOU ARE, IF YOU CHOOSE TO ACCEPT IT'. If your mind is programmed to do something in a certain way, to think in a certain way, you will get results in that certain way.

The good thing is, it is what others use to define you. Your creator did not put you in a box, he gave you the ability to express yourself in different ways. I believe that's the reason why you can take one of these questionnaires and sometimes have different results depending on what mood you are in, I know because I tried it.

The question is, how do you define yourself? And not how others define you!

Have you allowed yourself to be put into one of these boxes?

Does a specific personality box really apply to your life?

I went through the analysis myself and saw that I don't fit into just one of these boxes but many of them. I came to the realisation that when I was created, I was not created with limitations on my life so a set of personality traits can not contain me and the same applies to you.

Your creator is to big to be confined in a box. He has poured his Spirit into you, and as you carry his Spirit, you carry his personality and that means that you can not be confined into a personality box. Neither should you allow yourself to be confined into one. You can operate in all these personality traits and behaviours if you want to. You may fit into one category or you might fit into more than one, the truth is you are the only person that can determine your attitude, character, and habits.

Every human being is made up of a combination of the spirit person and the flesh person. Your spirit person sees the possibilities, while your flesh person focus on the obstacles that stop you from achieving things.

The systems of life that dictate how we live and operate on earth automatically programme our limiting belief thoughts. That's why if you believe you can't, automatically, you won't. That is why most of the things you wish to have in life have eluded you, because you have entertained the thought that they are beyond your reach. To achieve anything of significance requires an *attitude of positive attainment* and *a desire that is un-defeating.*

Everyone is guaranteed a good life the moment they were born. However, we have allowed our circumstances and environment to shape our portion in life. You are the only person that can decide your future, whether to create the direct path to your destiny or continue to go on the treadmill of life going nowhere.

Why You Were Sent To Earth For A Time As This?

'You are a piece in the Jigsaw puzzle of Life, find your place and fit in'.

You are the answer to someone's question for the generation that you find yourself in. It is a travesty that people go to their graves without answering their call. Your call is to be born, your call is to be relevant, your call is to fulfil your destiny and your destiny is to find your purpose in life and walk in it.

The American novelist and painter, Henry Miller put it like this;

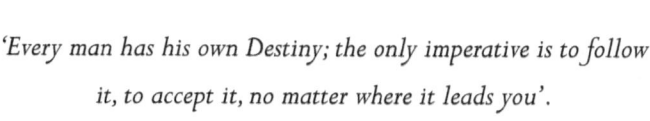

'Every man has his own Destiny; the only imperative is to follow it, to accept it, no matter where it leads you'.

It is important to answer the call that was placed on your life, it will benefit you as a person and your generation as a beneficiary of the great things you have to offer. No one is immune from trials and obstacles, however, the perseverance of searching and finding the question that you were called to answer is the most rewarding feeling in life. However, it's just the beginning of the journey of your life.

What do you Value?

What have you always wanted to do? What is that thing that you have a disposition to? What is that problem that you want to solve? What is it that gives you that greatest sense of satisfaction? What is that activity that will give you the greatest feeling of importance, and sense of well being? Whatever your answer is to these questions is an indication, a pointer, to who YOU really are. You are not anonymous with your purpose, 'Your Purpose is tied into Your Existence'. Your answers to the above questions will tie into your area of excellence. That is why you have the skill you have and a sense of dissatisfaction towards the subject when your mind entertains them. It is your responsibility to take ownership of the path that those thoughts are leading you to, work and walk in that direction to achieve the purpose set for you.

You will find what your purpose is in the journey of services you render to people and the problems you help bring a solution to. You are not required to solve every problem, you just have to solve the problem that has been assigned to you by your creator. We live in a simple, yet complex world made up of principles and laws, natural and man-made, generations have come and gone, but we are still discovering the beauties of creation. If you are not feeling fulfilled right now, it means you have not answered the question that you have been sent to earth to answer. It may be a small question or it may even be a big one, all I know is that only you can answer it and if you don't, you will be the one to give account to your creator for a life wasted.

Ralph Waldo Emerson said;

'The purpose of life is not to be happy, it is to be useful, to be honourable, to be compassionate, to make some difference and to have lived and lived well'.

I always get a tingle inside when watching the film, 'Saving Private Ryan'. When it comes to the end of the film when the character of Ryan makes his final statement to his wife which is, 'Have I lived a good life?' In other words he was saying, did I attain my destiny? Has my life been purposeful? Has my life counted for something? Did my generation benefit from me being on this earth? In his reflection of his life, he wanted to know whether he had earned the sacrifices that were made on his behalf. In the film, a group of soldiers sacrificed their lives to preserve his, those soldiers fulfilled their destiny, they fulfilled their call to duty, and Ryan was told to 'earn it'. I want to ask you today, have you discovered your reason for existence or are you still walking or jogging on the treadmill of life going nowhere?

As you are reading this book today, depending on where you are in your walk of life, ask yourself these questions; Have I led a good Life? Am I leading a purposeful life? Am I walking and living a destiny fulfilling life? Have I made my existence on earth count for something? All those that have gone before me, have I made their sacrifices count? Whatever your answers to these questions, no matter where you are in your life path, it is possible to make adjustments and reposition yourself onto the right path for YOU.

I say this because, I am living proof that it is possible to find who you are despite your age, religion, or sex. You can find out what your purpose in life is and take the necessary steps to start walking in it. I searched for some years, I tried different things, some costly, yet educative, and I came to the understanding that 'before you can truly find out who you are, you need to take time out from what you are doing'.

The great physicists and philosopher, Albert Einstein said,

'Problems can not be solved at the same level of awareness that created them'

The true understanding of that statement is; if you want to change a situation, you need to separate yourself from the situation so as to get a different perspective. That means, you need to withdraw yourself from your everyday life activities, going into your mind and slowing down all the activity that is going on in there and think.

There is a feeling of relaxation and relief you get from just slowing down, but the ultimate satisfaction comes when you find your purpose. At this point you have come to the realisation of your existence and the rewards that are attached to it.

There is no individual in history, that has not benefited from answering the call on their life. Bill Gates in software manufacturing, Thomas Edison in the discovery of the Light bulb, John Maxwell in teaching the discipline of Leadership, Sean Combs, better known as P Diddy, in the development and explosion of Rap and R&B music to the mainstream, Richard Branson, creating the Virgin brand to deliver better quality products and services at a cheaper cost to people. All these people are human beings like you and I. So, it is possible to give what is inside you for the benefit of your generation.

The only day you have is today, you only have today to decide about accepting who you have been called to be, because you are not promised tomorrow. As a person, you want somebody to say, 'my life is a little richer because you showed up on this planet'. Your creator made you so your life will count for something.

Find out who you are, master who you are and pour out who you are.

Key Learning Points:

1. You are on earth to solve a problem.
2. Only you can solve the problem you were created to solve.
3. Only you can find out who you are.
4. Only you can limit you.
5. There are rewards in fulfilling your purpose.
6. Changing your view of yourself is never too late, you can start right now.

Chapter 2

The Facts About You

'Let us make man in our image, make them reflecting our nature'

The Creator

There is something about a creator and his creation, a creator pours himself into what he is making. At some point in my life, I got into film and video editing and became an editor. I spent time perfecting the final edit to make it into a masterpiece that I can be proud of. I kept tweaking the video until there was nothing left to tweak in it. In generations past we have had various creators grace the earth, such as the likes of Leonardo Da Vinci, the creator of the world famous painting, the Mona Lisa. Another creator is Michael Angelo who carved the Statue of David; and not forgetting the grand inventor of them all Thomas A. Edison the creator of the electric light bulb as we know it today. When a creation lasts for so long, it shows how much the creator invested into it. There is one common factor in all the names mentioned above, they put their life into their works of art. When you create something, you create it out of love and passion, you build a relationship with it.

You were created by a creator who fashioned you in his image and in his likeness. Because your creator loved you, He poured his Spirit into you, causing you to have his attributes and his nature and the capability of creating your own masterpiece. It has been proven that it is only the human race that has the ability to reason, to use their mind to discern things. Every individual has a conscience that enables them to think and make decisions. St Augustine, put it like this;

*'Some people, in order to discover God, read books.
But there is a great book: the very appearance of created things.
Look above you! Look below you! Read it. God, whom you want
to discover, never wrote that book with ink. Instead
He set before your eyes the things that He had made. Can you
ask for a louder voice than that?'*

Chapter 2

Wow! Now that is something, the beautiful flowers, the waves of the sea, the fruit from the trees; there could not be a better statement of creation than what we visibly see.

Scientists have endeavoured to try and explain the origin of creation, but came to a dead end. Some agreed secretly that every creation came from a creator or a force, that is far greater than the created.

There have been various debates about creation. There is the Christian belief of the creation story according to the Bible and there is the humanistic belief of evolution.

In my case, I believe in creation and the fact that there is a creator. I find it very hard to understand, and why anyone else would for that matter, the thought of 'beauty coming out of chaos without any form of process', it is beyond my imagination, it goes against the laws of nature. Can you imagine what it would be like for your image to emerge from a lump of matter and from there continue to evolve, where would the beauty be?

God created YOU, plain and simple, you do not have to believe it, but it will be beneficial for your present and eternity if you do. God created you in his image and formed you in his likeness and that gives you the characteristics of God and it makes you God-like. That is why for a split second you can consider having the good things in life, that is why your spirit can wonder into nature, and that is why it is easy for you to love because your creator is love.

Your creator had and still has a plan for your life. The fact that you are reading this book, means that you want to know the plan concerning your life. This book will take you on a journey of revelation and enlightenment of the truths that lay dormant inside you. If you did not believe there was another side to who you are, you would not experience the agitations of feeling that you should be achieving more than you are. With that in mind, why don't we try and get into the mind of our creator and see what these plans are and let us start working towards living a more fulfilled life.

This book is not a discussion about creation, however, I believe that life, as I know it, came from the creator, Almighty God. He created every human being in his image, and every human being he created was good until the sin of man entered the equation. The connection man had with his creator was cut off. This explains all the elements of negativity that we experience on a daily basis, these negative elements play a major part in our everyday life.

After the disconnection, the first negative attribute or emotion we hear about is fear. Man became fearful of his creator and distanced himself from him. This fear has permeated through the rest of creation at birth, that is why it is easy for you to fear situations and circumstances that you face.

Your creator created you so your life would count. He created you for goodness and put his life into you that is why you have thoughts that are good. However, the negativity in our environment suppresses the positive thoughts we have. The great philosopher, Ralph Waldo Emerson said and I quote:

"The purpose of life is not to be happy. It is to be useful, to be honourable, to be compassionate, to have it make some difference that you have lived and lived well."

Your creator put so much emphasis in your design, so you can fit the specification of the problem you are meant to solve.

The Created

Take stock of yourself; your body, your mind, your heart and your spirit. You have different abilities in order to achieve different results.

Your Spirit

The information and data you allow into your mind can help you become who you are called to be or it can help you be who you allow yourself to be.

Your spirit, which you received from your creator, contains what makes you who you are. It is this spirit that attracts you to the good things in life such as a happy family life, a good home, a good car and a fulfilled life. However, all these things do not come easy and sometimes they do not come at all; even if you have all these things you still want more. If you have not found who you really are you need to reconnect with the spirit that created you.

The key to who you are called to be is locked up inside your spirit. It is this key that will lift all the burdens of life that you experience, it is this key that will enable you to identify and discern the different personalities that live within you.

Your Body

Your physical body is your outer shell, it is the part of you that people see. Your personality is closely related and strongly attached to your physical body from birth. After the disconnection from the creator, everyone that was born of a woman and came into this world, was born into a world of negativity, fear, strife, lust, poverty, and death.

This is the part of you that lives in the 'can not do' area of life. The voices that tell you, 'I can not afford that, I can not do that, that will never happen for me', is the part of you that lives in the atmosphere of fear, doubt and poverty. This is the you that stops you from exploring the possibilities of life. This is when you start having the thoughts of failure and most of the time you get what you ask for. It's the part of you that thinks of all the negative things that you do not want but, you always seem to experience. Things like greed, impossibilities, and sickness. The flip side to this negativity is the positive you, the part of you that thinks of self-development, self-realisation and self-awareness. The you that thinks of the positive things in life such as good health, unlimited wealth, unlimited possibilities, love, and friendship. It is this positive self-awareness that can help you attain the master key to being the you that your creator created you to be.

At creation everything that was created was good and beautiful. The 'created' knew who he was. However, when sin entered the world, the God-created system was turned upside down, fear took over from faith and hence the created had a self-image problem. The created questioned their existence in their creator.

I do not know where you are in your relationship with your creator, but since the redemption of man, there has been a reconnection opportunity between the creator and the created. That is why you can experience the attributes of love; kindness, empathy, the power to create, the power to live a fulfilled and successful life. You have the keys to reconnect to your purpose in life, they are located inside you. For you to get them out requires you to be still and dig deep inside of you. The spirit that created you is of God because God breathed his spirit into you. It is that spirit that made you a living being, it made you of God stock. When you reconnect to him, you become like him and you begin to carry his nature inside you. Successful people that have gone before you, have acknowledged the existence of a greater power, a greater source, the creator of all mankind. They have discovered themselves and have done so by coming into contact with their inner self, they have programmed their mind to give to their generation as the creator instructed them to.

God said to Jeremiah in the Bible; 'before I shaped you in the belly of your mother, I knew you' if your creator knew Jeremiah, a created person, the same applies to you. It is so amazing that your creator had a plan for your life even before you were created. He didn't just slap up a couple of cells to form your fetus. Your God knew beforehand what he wanted you to do when you arrived on earth, and he placed it inside of you. Your future was planned out to deliver a package to your generation; you are under obligation to seek out your purpose in life and make your portion of this generation to be a better place.

The Plan

The task of fully reconnecting to our purpose and destiny is not easy. It has taken years of environmental mind programming to condition our minds to the attributes that it operates under. It is impossible and highly unlikely to expect an overnight transformation in behaviour, attitude, belief system and, mind power. This kind of transformation will take dedication, commitment, will power and desire. There will be trials and errors as you go along the way, but if you commit to your plan of finding your true identity, you will find it. Your spirit will need to be completely identified with the spirit of your creator. You need to acknowledge the fact that you come from a greater source of life, that you are on this earth for a purpose. You have a mission to accomplish: Thomas S. Monson, the President of the Church of Jesus Christ of Latter-day Saints said;

'I acknowledge that I do not understand the process of creation, but I accept the fact of it'.

It is not your responsibility to understand how your environment came in to being. You just need to key into the fact that nature exists and generates a source of energy and force that is bigger than you. Along the way you might have the revelation of eternity and the pathway to it.

On my journey of self-realisation and self-awareness, I was well versed in all the theory of finding who you are. I prayed, I tried things, I delved into religious stuff, men!

I got busy, I worked, I trained, but nothing. Then I took time away from all the stuff that was making me busy, I went into a period of praying, waiting and listening for an answer; remember, I said, praying, waiting and listening for an answer and then it came.

In life, we keep running around doing stuff and not taking time to be still, to appreciate what is around us, or to find out what is in us. We just continue to be busy doing the things that do not impact our generation and in being busy, we tend to loose focus and struggle our way through life and achieve close to nothing and die.

My creator, revealed to me, something that I had been doing eighteen years ago, as being my purpose. Believe it or not, when I looked back and reviewed my life to get clarity, it all fell into place. As I said at the beginning of this book, it was the missing jewel in my crown and at the point of realisation, my heart was filled with absolute joy. At that moment I knew that my life had now found its focus and I can start walking in the direction of achieving my purpose in life.

Despite my destiny and purpose being right in front of me, I was blinded by my surroundings and environment.

I was clouded by the less important things in life. I even retrained myself in a new university degree, believing that it was my destiny. Little did I know that the new degree I acquired was a mere tool and a training platform for me to reach out to my purpose in life.

I believe, the view of the creator is the best view to have. his view makes everything seem easy and attainable. It makes the long journeys seem short. It is in your time of struggle, that your creator will carry you and help you through those times of difficulty. He said in his word that he will never leave you or forsake you. You are bound to go through turbulent times in life, look at Thomas Edison, he failed ten thousand times before he had a breakthrough. Imagine, trying something and continuously failing at it over and over and over again, yet still keeping at it. I do not know what belief he had, or how in tune he was with his creator, but what I do know is God only allows a thing in its time, and things can be a lot smoother with Him than without Him.

You will only be able to see, when you are fully focused; and the best place to have your initial focus on, is your creator. He is the author, creator and originator of your faith.

You need to re-establish that connection that will allow you to tap into the mysteries of the creator. This will enable you to draw out the wisdom and knowledge that will give you an edge; an easy path in connecting with your destiny and finding your purpose in life.

Key Learning Points

1. Your creator has a plan for your life.
2. Your creator planned you life purpose and destiny before you were formed in your mother's womb.
3. You have to re-establish the connection between your spirit and that of your creator.
4. Everyone has the capability of creating a masterpiece.

Chapter 3

Your Attitude

'You Are The Architect Of Your Failure Or Success'

Your Attitude

The power to find who you are is in your ability to maintain a positive mental attitude. Your outlook on life is formed from your perception of it. Two men were travelling a 60 mile journey, one said, 'we've only gone 30 miles', the other says, 'we only have 30 miles to go'. It is all in the attitude, some people see a cup half empty, while others see the same cup half full, it's all in the attitude.

Whether you like it or not, your attitude is a major player in your everyday life. You determine your lot in life through your attitude. Most of the time it is your attitude that makes the impossible possible. Former heavyweight boxing champion of the world and sportsman of the century, Mohammed Ali said,

'To be a great champion you must believe you are the best. If you are not, pretend you are'.

That definitely worked for him against George Foreman in their heavyweight fight back in 1974.

Whatever You Believe You Will Achieve

When I was growing up, I loved to watch boxing; my hero in the ring was Mohammed Ali. In boxing, the one most crucial thing that defines whether a fighter has the winning edge is not his talent, it's in his attitude. You get a winning edge from a positive attitude, but it needs to be constantly fed with positive thoughts and affirmations to maintain its positivity.

I try to follow the different boxing divisions whenever I can, however my favourite is the heavyweight division. Lets take a look at these two great boxing legends Mohammed Ali and Mike Tyson:

Mohammed Ali, born Cassius Marcellus Clay, Jr,; January 17, 1942. He was voted the Sports personality of the Century by the British Broadcasting Corporation (BBC) and also Sports man of the century by Sports Illustrated. Ali was defeated on five occasions in his professional career, a three-time heavyweight champion, a husband, a father, a grandfather, an activist and an entertainer. Throughout history there have been great boxers, but Ali was different. He was positive in his outlook and attitude, he did not believe in loosing. Some of his quotes were so comical and this attracted people to him. I went through so many quotes of this great athlete, yet I could not find one where he spoke negatively about himself. In one of his interviews he said;

'I wrestled with an alligator, I done tussled with a whale; handcuffed lightning, thrown thunder in jail; only last week, I murdered a rock, injured a stone, hospitalised a brick; I'm so mean I make medicine sick' (1974).

Even when he failed his army aptitude test in 1964 he said, 'I said I was the greatest not the smartest', and it was this attitude that was key to a lot of his successes in life. Yes, he had troubles, struggles, and failed occasionally in his path of life, but there is one trait that could not be taken away from him; he identified early in his life that a positive mental attitude can take him along way. Even when all was against him, he still believed in himself and came through the fight in 1974 tagged 'the Rumble in the Jungle'. I believe he believed in himself so much, that he did not see the impossibilities that were in front of him.

Lets look at what was before him; George Foreman, younger, stronger, had knocked out the two fighters that had previously taken Ali the distance and beaten him by decisions. Even his close associates didn't believe he could win, yet, against all odds, he overcame the mountain before him and achieved his goal. I do not know of any other boxer like Ali and I am not sure we will ever see another like him, but, I have learnt from him that your attitude plays a major role in overcoming impossible mountains.

Mike Tyson was the most fearsome fighter in his era, they called him Iron Mike. He was the youngest ever heavyweight champion, he put fear into most of his opponents before he even landed a punch. He didn't talk much during or after the fights. I read up on his early years, the struggles he faced, and some of the quotes attributed to him. I felt there was a sense of self battle within him and despite winning the heavyweight belts, his attitude to life and his surroundings was not the best, to say the least.

I believe, this affected his career, which was cut short due to various reasons and these battles sent him into the boxing wilderness. Mike Tyson allowed his environment, his associates, and his personality to cloud his attitude towards life, and it affected him in a negative manner. He allowed these factors to ride on him instead of him riding on them and that led to his world being disrupted by personal problems and indiscipline issues.

What is Attitude?

Your attitude is defined as the way a person views an issue or thing, be it negative or positive. The French author, Tom Blandi put it like this;

'Our attitudes control our lives, attitudes are a secret power working twenty-four hours a day, for good or bad. It is of paramount importance that we know how to harness and control this great force'.

The dictionary defines *attitude* as; a complex mental state involving beliefs, feelings, values and dispositions to act in certain ways.

Your attitude can open doors for you and on the flip side can shut doors against you. Your life is as a result of cause and effect. Through out your life, you are causing something that will yield a ripple effect, which is in reaction to the cause. Your attitude determines your approach to life and often enough, your attitude determines whether you will be successful or not. Your attitude determines the way in which people approach you. You have total control over your attitude and it helps if you maintain a good one.

Formation of Your Attitude

What forms your attitude? The attitude you have today is a result of various influences from birth and development over the years. Your attitude is formed and shaped through different attributes, circumstances, and factors in your life. If you have a negative attitude towards life, it is bound to affect your outcome and your relationships in life. So whatever you set out to do, if in a negative attitude, it will yield negative results. On the other hand whatever you set yourself to do in a positive attitude, is bound to yield positive results. The difference between a problem and an opportunity in life, is the attitude used in viewing the situation. Finding problems to solve gives you an opportunity to identify your purpose in life, and the assignment your creator assigned to you.

The attitude you have today is a result of your own doing. You were not born with the attitude, however, you have formed yourself into it. The good thing is, you can change it. Although, it can sometimes fluctuate, being negative and sometimes positive; you do not have to die with it, you can always improve on your attitude.

If you are constantly surrounded by people with a negative outlook on life and they continue to talk about negative things, you will most likely have a negative attitude towards life. Remember, attitudes are contagious.

If you have negative thoughts towards your ambitions and dreams, you will almost certainly live a limited life with no possibilities; you will always see the obstacles and focus on them. However, if you have a positive attitude, you will see the same obstacles as opportunities and stepping stones to success and greatness. Ultimately, the keys are in your hands; you determine your success or failure, you can choose to be a winner or you can choose to be a loser.

Factors That Influence The Formation Of An Attitude

These various factors contribute to our attitude and eventually who we become outwardly.

Environment

When I was growing up, I saw a lot of poverty and it framed my mind to not think bigger than my environment. If I saw a nice beautiful house, the first thing that came to my mind was 'I would like to have that, but that is impossible, there is no way I can have it'. Your environment develops the types of beliefs you take forward in life whether negative or positive. These beliefs re-enforce your attitude and mould the person you become. As often as not, it's these attitudes that are formed at the beginning of your life that are the hardest to change.

The foundational attitudes we have, stem from our environment and surroundings. These attitudes become embedded in us up to our teen years and early adult life. Our environment plays a major part in the formation of our attitudes in the early part of our lives. It is at the stage of early development, children gradually start to form different beliefs and philosophies about themselves. Despite the different characteristics that we might have possessed at birth and our early years, what we see around us plays a major role in our development as a person.

What you see around you, what is fed into your mind, shapes you into who you eventually become.

Opinions

The words people say about you, as well as the words said to you can seriously affect your attitude. words can scar you internally. They can bring a sense of rejection if negative and a sense of affection if positive. Our words can be like daggers to the heart or like sweet honey in our mouth.

Affirmation

You are more interested in how someone feels towards you than anything else. It is a key factor that forms your attitude. When you are told that you are loved and appreciated, it goes a long way to making you feel good and enriched. On the other hand no affirmation can lead to an attitude of not being appreciated.

Personality

Who am I? Our personality shapes our attitude. We were all born with a distinct personality from any other person. Even identical twins have different personalities and each personality has an identifying temperament that is reflected in your attitude.

Self Image

At the stage of adulthood, self image is important in the construction or re-construction process of forming a positive attitude. If we see ourselves in a negative way, we set a time bomb of self destruction. Mike Tyson said;

'I just look around and say, I'm a mess, I don't know why I do things and I know I'm going to blow one day. My life is doomed the way it is: I have no future'.

We all know what happened to him, he lost his titles, he lost his wife, he lost his wealth and his freedom. The heart of every person has the capacity to love itself and this is a good thing when it does not extend to selfishness.

Associations

The people we associate with such as colleagues, family, peers, and friends affect our attitudes in the way we deal with them. I work in various teams and it is so painful listening to the negative words that come out of the mouth of colleagues when they come back from holiday; 'I hate this place', welcome back to hell'.

It is funny when you dislike your environment, but expect to have a good time in it. Some of my colleagues feel their environment is hell, then they wonder why they are dissatisfied with their jobs.

Most of the time we try and conform our attitudes to that of people around us such as friends, colleagues, peers, and religious group members. We build a belief that; if our attitudes match that of the person we are basing it on, then we must be correct. However, that is never the case, your attitude is specific to you and only you should be the one to build it based on a positive belief system.

Appearance

A persons attitude can be shaped by a persons appearance. Society has created the opinion and view that the way you look determines the kind of person you are. The media have focused on the size of the parts of your body or your height. Even your looks have been used to define your attitude to the extent that peoples salaries have been determined by height. In a survey a few years ago, it showed that tall men receive a higher salary than short men. Your physical appearance can affect your attitude. The world of media is setting the pace in development and also in shaping peoples attitudes due to the images portrayed as trend setters. Conditioning the mind to follow the trends that they see in media. We compare ourselves to these images on television, on the internet and in magazines; so we can see whether our attitude conforms to social reality and acceptability or not.

Attitude Analysis

It is easy to chart your destiny if you have a good positive attitude towards life. Whatever you show to the world is what the world will use in reply to you. If you are nice to people, people will be nice to you and in the same way, if you are horrible to people, they will in turn be horrible to you. You can't sow corn and expect to reap tomatoes, that is against the natural laws of the universe. The same universal laws apply to our attitude, you determine what you get in life through your attitude. With Ali, he attained greatness and the love of the people beyond measure with his contagious positive attitude, while Tyson experienced some uncomfortable times in his life.

Before you can be ready for your assignment, your attitude needs to be right with yourself, your family, your surroundings and especially your creator. If you sow love in your attitude, you will receive love back.

Negative Attitude Analysis

Our attitudes are built over a period of time and are an evaluation of the various aspects of our environment, which influence our behaviour and our thoughts. Harbouring a negative attitude can cause adverse reactions from people, because they perceive the negativity that comes from a negative attitude.

Six Dangers of a Negative Attitude

1. **A Negative Attitude Creates Doubt:** People with a negative attitude always see the reason why something cannot be done. They are the people that always see the obstacle and not the opportunity. They are the people who always blame others for things that go wrong with them.

2. **A Negative Attitude turns a Pile of Sand into a big Mountain:** People with a negative attitude always make drama out of every situation. They fail to see the possibilities, instead all they can see are the impossibilities.

3. **A Negative Attitude Limits Your ability to enjoy the good things in life:** People with a negative attitude are more focused on things to go wrong, than for things to go right. Even your creator has given you all the earth to enjoy, but a negative attitude stops you from enjoying it.

4. **A Negative Attitude Negatively Affects the People Around You:** People with negative attitudes make everyone around them miserable. A negative attitude is contagious like a cold.

5. **A Negative Attitude Limits Divine Intervention in Your life:** People with negative attitudes limit the possibilities that can happen through the external force that combines with applied human faith.

6. **A Negative Attitude Keeps You from the Revelation of the True You:** People with a negative attitude build up a barrier between them and their creator. A negative attitude is the opposite of faith, it takes faith to believe and understand the mysteries of the creator of heaven and earth. Without faith it is impossible to please Him.

For you to find out your true identity you need to have a positive mental attitude. No one has achieved anything meaningful without a positive mental attitude.

A positive mental attitude is what allows you to be creative, it helps you find inner wisdom, it also helps you breakdown barriers. It is the first key to finding who you are.

As human beings, our minds are programmed for failure, fear, limitation and poverty. You need to exercise your mind to think positive thoughts. You need to think of things you want and not things you don't want. The mind attracts itself to things it feeds itself with. A positive mental attitude will make you see an opportunity in an obstacle. The forming of a positive attitude helps a great deal in being successful in your endeavours.

For you to enjoy your life, you need a renewal of attitude. The mind has been programmed over the years with all the natural established attitudes of various beliefs, opinions convictions, prejudices, thoughts and ideas.

There is a way of renewing your mind and that is through positive thinking; replacing negative thoughts with positive thoughts. For instance, the things you see as obstacles, start seeing them as opportunities. You might have be given lemons in life, try and make lemonade or lemon juice. Obstacles are a necessity encountered on a regular basis, and are presented before you for you to overcome, or for you to re-direct your path in your journey of life. If an obstacle is placed before you, it will take energy and effort to overcome it, once the obstacle is overcome, the reward is invaluable. If an obstacle can not be overcome, then it enables you to make a decision to seek another path, it takes a positive attitude to view an obstacle as an opportunity.

Thomas A. Edison didn't see his ten thousand failures as obstacles, he simply saw them as opportunities of getting closer to his dream of inventing the electric bulb. As did every time Henry Ford tried the mass production process for manufacturing cars for the public before the model T car revolutionised the way of life of early America. And what about Bill Gates who revolutionised the way we use computers today with Microsoft software. All these successful individuals saw the obstacles before them as opportunities and took them head-on.

There is always an opportunity to change your attitude and you can start the process today, you can start right now.

These are four steps to transforming your attitude:

1. Step out of your box

Albert Einstein said;

'The significant problems we face can not be solved by the same level of thinking that created them'

In other words, the mind that see's something as an obstacle can not turn it into an opportunity, you have to renew your thought process. You first need to identify where you are. Second, find out what is going on in your mind. Thirdly, step out from yourself, detach yourself from your current reality, your current mindset; after this and only after this can you start walking the path to self renewal. This initial exercise takes you to a higher psychological level where the change you are seeking can take place.

2. Identify the thoughts of the things you don't want

Natural thoughts sound like – 'I don't want to be poor, I don't want to be fat, I don't like shopping, I don't like this, I don't like that'. Even as you have indicated that you don't want these things, but because your thought process has considered these thoughts, your mind is programmed to associate with these factors.

3. Fill your mind with positive thoughts

For your attitude to be transformed, you need to focus your mind on positive things, focus your mind on the things you want in life.

You need to fill your mind with 'I want' thoughts. Thoughts such as 'I want to be rich, I want to be healthy, I want to be successful' and then you feed these new thoughts with a burning desire for them to come to fruition in your life, for these thoughts to become your reality. You need to engrave these desires onto your subconscious mind.

Get Your whole Being Involved

The whole of your being: your body, your heart, your mind and your spirit need to be in total agreement to bring these new positive thoughts into your reality. Creating a burning desire for this change is very important; you need to want these things so bad and be willing to give anything for it.

Rewards of a Positive Attitude

A Positive Attitude helps you keep a Limitless Belief System

When you have a positive attitude, your mind does not entertain limited beliefs. You always have a positive outlook on life. Where the people around you see problems, you see possibilities.

A Positive Attitude leads you to your purpose in life

With a positive attitude, you are able to believe there is more to life than waking up, going to work or school, coming home and going to sleep and eventually growing old, then death. A positive attitude helps you decide that you are going to attain your purpose in life, it helps you to apply your mind and attain success in life. When you focus on a positive outlook to life your creator will ignite passions inside you that will reveal your true purpose.

Levy Roots, creator of the *Reggae Reggae* sauce brand in the United Kingdom, changed his attitude completely from an ex-convict into a dragon slayer on the Dragon's den to receive investment capital for his creation of a spiced sauce that can make very bland food taste spicy and delicious. He decided in his darkest hour that he did not have to be who he was, because he had the power to be who his creator had called him to be. He found his niche, he found what made him tick, he found his passion and has turned it into a million pound passion.

Chapter 3

A Positive Attitude opens doors of favour to you

When you operate with a positive attitude, people will embrace you, warm to you, open up to you and will even connect you to opportunities that will benefit you. It happens all the time, it comes out of the trust habit that has developed from your reaction to them.

Last year, I took a trip to Africa. Upon arriving at the airport, I had to wait for my driver to pick me up from the lobby area. I sat next to an elderly gentleman, we exchanged greetings, he was waiting for his driver too. He tried to call them but his phone was not going through for some reason, so I offered him my phone to make the call, I did not think anything of it. Soon after he finished the call, he asked me what I was doing back in Africa, I said that I was looking for different opportunities to benefit my business and community. He was impressed and said that it is good when young people take time to think about nation building and development. Soon enough his driver arrived, he thanked me for the assistance and gave me his card and said anytime I am in town I should call upon him. Little did I know when I looked at the card, he was a traditional ruler of a town, and I just offered him my phone to make a simple call.

All the people mentioned above are real, they have two legs, one brain, two hands, they are black, they are white. Attitude does not discriminate, it does not care who you are.

key learning points

1. You need a positive attitude to identify your purpose in life.
2. You have the power to change your attitude.
3. There are rewards for having a positive attitude.
4. Your attitude is contagious.
5. What you see around you, what is fed into your mind, shapes you into who you eventually become.

Chapter 4

Habit And Character

'Character: Your Key to Sustainability'

Your character is shaped by your habits and behaviours. Your character is the sum of qualities that show up in your ethical strength, it describes your attributes and traits. Your character is the bedrock of your being, it is what your attitude springs from. Your character acts as the foundation from where your attitude starts to build your reputation on, for the view of the outside world.

John Wooden, legendary head coach of the UCLA Bruins basketball team put it this way;

'Be more concerned with your character than your reputation, because your character is what you really are, while your reputation is merely what others think you are'.

That statement is so true, when everything is stripped away, money, fame, attitude, it takes character for a man or woman to get back up and start it all over again.

The great evangelist Billy Graham put it like this;

'When wealth is lost nothing is lost, when health is lost something is lost, when character is lost all is lost'.

It takes men and women of character to build a nation, to build a society, to build a home.

Our habits build our character positively or negatively; it is our habitual behaviour that our subconscious mind uses as building blocks. Your behaviour creates for you a value system that you judge yourself by, and others judge you by as well. To positively build your character you need to evaluate your value system, check your habits, understand what a habit is and how it is formed.

Achievers in life have a sound character. This comes from monitoring the habits they allow to shape their character. When you are able to exchange bad habits for good habits, you start on to the path of sound character building and a disciplined life.

Habit: What it is

A habit is simply what you do on a regular basis without thinking about it. A habit is what you know to do, how you know to do, and why you do or want to do. Breaking this down further; a habit is something that you do and have the knowledge and skill to do it plus the fact that you want to do it.

What to do – Knowledge
How to do – Skill
Why to do or want to do – Attitude

A habit needs to have the three ingredients of what, how and why or want for it to be formed in the mind of a person. Habits can be classified into good habits or bad habits, it is these that you do over and over again that form your behavioural pattern and eventually build your character. Controlling your habits are very important as they guide the path to your destination in life, be it success or failure.

Good Habits

An example of a potentially good habit is, to exercise for one hour everyday or reading a self development book every month. These two examples could be considered good habits because reading a self development book will improve your knowledge about yourself and will help you develop yourself within. Exercising for an hour everyday will help you live a healthy life.

Bad Habits

A bad habit is a habit that can be seen as negative to a person and can yield detrimental effects. A habit that can yield such effects is not washing your hands after using the toilet, which can lead to the spread of germs and most definitely sickness. Another bad habit can be smoking, which can cause lung cancer and eventually death. If you consistently get yourself into trouble, you build a habit of bad behaviour which results in a character of indiscipline, which can result in a stint of jail time.

Formation of Habits

Habits are learned over a period of time. Good habits take effort to learn while bad habits are not so difficult to pick up. Our mind is programmed to attract habits that require less effort in doing and it does not take a lot of effort to be untidy, unhygienic, and/or undisciplined. It is said that anything worth doing is worth doing well. When you wake up from bed, you go and brush your teeth, this is a positive habit because it is a preventive measure against tooth decay. This is embedded into you from childhood. However, if as a child there was no one available to monitor your daily dental hygiene, and now as an adult you do not brush your teeth in the morning because you don't feel like it, you have adopted the character trait of un-cleanliness.

This is simply obeying the law of cause and effect, which has gone on over the ages, and is the basis of all natural laws. For every effect there is a cause; simply put, what ever you sow you will reap: so if you sow no brushing you will reap bad breath and decayed teeth, while on the other hand if you sow regular brushing you will have good teeth and fresh breath, it is as simple as that. However, before you can come to an understanding of this principle it is one that needs to be taught and learnt. That's why most habits are learned as children, whether good or bad Habits may be learnt through direct teaching and learning or indirect learning, which might be through observation of parents or peers.

A habit can also be formed through practice and reward. Every human being would like to be rewarded, if you do something good like giving up your seat on a bus or train for an elderly person you enjoy the warmth that comes from the elderly person towards you or as in the case of brushing your teeth. The human psyche exhibits a desire for pleasure rather than suffering or pain. That is the reason why and how habits are formed, this the bedrock of habit formation. Once this principle is established in your mind, you will be able to change your habits from being negative to what you want them to be.

A good proven way is to reward yourself after making a habit change, I call it 'celebrate your successes'. This process can help you to quickly create a new set of behaviour patterns and burn them into your mind. Your thoughts become your words, your words become your actions, your actions become your habits and your habits become your character. Ultimately your character leads you to your destination in life.

Breaking the Bad Habits in Your Life with Rewards

Psychologists have performed various experiments and have come up with the knowledge that the best way to improve a habit or change a habit is through the reward system. When I was young, if I finish my chores my mother would reward me with a pound every week. This has allowed me to continue this process in my personal life in rewarding myself when I accomplish a task.

Breaking the Bad Habits in Your Life withholding Rewards

As you can break habits through rewarding, you can also break habits through not rewarding and withholding a reward. My dad use to stop me from going to play football with my friends whenever I did not finish my assignments from school.

Breaking the Bad Habits in Your Life with Punishment

Another way which experts have proved to be the least effective is to punish yourself or a person as a measure in breaking bad habits. When you associate pain with a habit, you tend to avoid it.

In the case of the reward system the brain undergoes a conditioning, to reflect the new habit that has been acquired.

The use of the reward system to change habits is a way of conditioning the mind and associating the habit with the reward offered as compensation. This form of habit building is the most successful when you are trying to transform your habits. There are three types of reward criteria when compensating for a habit transformation: there is the intermittent rewarding, the deferred rewarding, or immediate rewarding.

Intermittent Rewarding

This aspect of rewarding requires you to reward randomly for certain activities achieved. I remember when I was young, I would always visit the chicken shop when coming from school. After I placed my order, I would go over to the Star Wars slot machine. The funny thing was sometimes I won and sometimes I lost, but most of the time I ended up spending more money than I won whenever I left with my chicken. That is exactly how the intermittent rewarding process operates; you continue to perform the new habit and on occasion you reward yourself for a job well done. It serves as a treat for yourself and a celebration for conquering the previous bad habit.

Deferred Rewarding

Deferred rewarding is a system that defers any reward to the future. This can be the promise to buy yourself a big present if major success is achieved in a goal or target set for yourself such as; the achievement of financial management goals, weight loss, eating healthy, as well as the goal to stop smoking. This type of rewarding is an outstanding way to build habits and achieve goals in other areas of your life and has been known to be used regularly by successful achievers.

Immediate Rewarding

This type of rewarding system is done immediately after an activity has occurred and is completed. It is seen that there is more gratification when you are rewarded immediately and the effect on you is greater. This type of reward system is used in building habits among children. Every week my children come home with awards from school. Their head teacher has created a system of rewarding his students for exhibiting various good habits. He embedded the system into the structure of the school; it motivates the children to build good habits. As a testament to the head teacher, the school is among the top fifty in the country and the best in the county.

In my opinion, the most effective reward system is deferred rewarding. It helps you set long term or short term goals, as well as allows you to plan ahead, and promotes focus and self-discipline. This method has worked for me in my personal life, I have achieved various goals using this process. It encouraged longevity in my habit and character building, these systems can be used for yourself or with your children.

Consistent habits build your character, however, maintaining your character gives you credibility.

Character Ethic

Your character is who you are, it is the summation of qualities that show up in a person. It is also the seat of power for your morals.

Your character is what your personality feeds off, it is an aspect of your life that all other aspects are built on. Your character gives a foundation to your personality and attitude, which is the outward projection of a person.

Abraham Lincoln said;

'Character is like a tree and reputation like a shadow. The shadow is what we think of it, the tree is the real thing'.

Chapter 4

People do not see your character, they only see your reputation. Our reputation is what we are in public, what people perceive us to be, while our character is who we are in private. That time when no one sees you, that time when you are building your character blocks with what you do daily, the different habits you have formed over the years. What character are you building today? What character have you already built over the years? What character did you build but you have diverted from? Depending on your answers to these questions, it is always possible to build again, it is possible to change direction.

There was a great man born in the year 1958 in Content, Clarendon Parish, Jamaica. He grew up with his grand parents and that's where his character was first shaped. He eventually travelled to England and before you know it, he got caught up in the crowd, lost his way and went to prison. But that's not the end of the story. While in prison, he traced his steps back to his original character, and once he came out of prison, he started his life afresh. He still held on to what his grand parents imparted in to him and from this, he continued to do what he knew best, which was to cook and play music. He began selling his sauce at the Notting Hill Carnival from 1991 to 2005. He got the opportunity to go on UK's popular TV show, The Dragon's Den, with the same character that was imparted into him from his grand parents. He got an investment of £50,000 and today, the young man then known as Keith Valentine Graham, is the multi-millionaire, Entrepreneur, Musician, Cookbook Author and Motivational Speaker Levi Roots.

From an early age, Levi's grand parents taught him the discipline of cooking and music. These two disciplines, formed the habits in his life that formed part of his character. Being the lead singer of a successful reggae group; whenever they were on tour, Levi said, he would always be in the kitchen, whipping up something and spicing it up to give it that West Indian flavour. Little did he know then, that these disciplines would be what would turn into a full blown business enterprise and turn him into a millionaire.

Our character sustains us through life. If you plan to do anything of real value in life, you need a positive attitude, and a credible character based on good and positive habits.

Your character is comprised of various attributes. It is these attributes that will determine the level of achievement you experience in the goals you set out for yourself.

More often than not, a change in your character is needed for you to be able to achieve goals you set for yourself. If you set a goal to become a successful writer and you have not been able to attain that goal, it could be that your goal is not in sync with your character attributes, which are suppose to drive you to achieving it.

Personality versus Character

Sometimes people get the two mixed up, but there is a variation. Your personality is the you that is projected to the outside world, the you that people see, the you that is made up from birth and part of your surroundings. Let me give you an example; your personality can be expressed as shy, confident, aggressive, rebellious, etc. These are traits associated with behaviour and are expressed outwardly. However, your character is a set of values that have been built, learned, and acquired over a period of time. These traits are what people do not see, but are there all the time. It is who you see in the mirror when you wake up. It is your character that sees you through the difficult phases you go through in life, character traits such as honesty, trustworthiness, respect, responsibility, dishonesty etc.

Because character is learned, it makes it possible to learn new habits that will help you build a different character of yourself.

Character Traits

Your character is formed from the blend of your personal and social character traits.

Personal Character Traits

Your personal character traits are formed from the attitudes you build towards activities, this is normally shown through your response to various challenges you come across. These character traits can either be positive or negative and maybe sometimes in between, however, whatever the traits that you build up into your personality, will determine your level of success or failure in life. An example of personal character traits are: Confidence, Courage, Determination, Hardworking, Careless, Diligent, Energetic, Lazy, etc. Your character is built over time from the different influences around you such as your parents, guardians, uncles, aunts, friends and peers. Most traits, if not all, are developed by associating with people and your environment. If you associate yourself with ambitious people, you will build an ambitious character because you will want to feel a sense of belonging amongst your peers. On the other hand, if your parents kept telling you that you could not do something from an early age, you will build a character of discouragement whenever a task that seems difficult is put before you.

John Locke, the seventeenth century English philosopher said;

'We are like chameleons, we take our hue and the colour of our moral character, from those who are around us'.

In John's case, as the father of liberalism and one of the most enlightened thinkers of his time, he should know.

The list of traits above is not exhaustive but they are some of the traits you should be looking out for in yourself. These positive and negative personal traits can determine your destination in life. No change in your environment or your circumstances can fix a defective or negative character, that decision needs to come from you. The beauty of it is your character is learned, you were not born with it so you definitely do not have to die with it, you can change it with some effort.

Social Character Traits

Your social character traits deal with how you interact with the people around you as well as people you come in contact with. These traits may be positive or negative. Positive social character traits have been known widely to lead to more fulfilling relationships with spouses, parents, friends and peers. On the other hand, negative social character traits have a tendency to lead to frustration, distrust and dislike in your relationships. Social character traits include but are not limited to the following: Fairness, Consideration, Reliability, Cruelty, Honesty, Dishonesty, Fairness, and Bias. Outside influences have a heavy impact on building the character of people. An example of someone that was affected by outside influence was Mike Tyson, former undisputed heavyweight boxing champion of the world, who was arrested thirty eight times before he was thirteen. I read, his father left his mother when he was two years old, his mother had to look after him, his brother and his sister till she passed away when Mike was sixteen. This shows how your environment can influence your character. However, at the age of sixteen, when his mother died he came under the influence of Cus D'Amato and Kevin Rooney, boxing trainer and manager. Cus D'Amato became his legal guardian, and his character traits were being transformed from what they were in his teen years, to characters traits of discipline and hard work.

If you have the wrong people around you, you will have the tendency to slip back into old habits and this was clearly evident in the life of Mike. When Cus D'Amato died and he parted ways with his manager and trainer Bill Clayton and Kevin Rooney, everything went downhill from there. What can be learned from this is the importance of continually feeding a new developed habit, so it will develop and become a sound character trait in you.

Your Character

How do you see yourself?

If you were asked to analyse your own character, I am sure you will find something positive to say. It is in our human nature to speak well of ourselves, unless the person has a mental or emotional problem that he or she is dealing with. Whatever character trait you exhibit, you are bound to see a positive side to it, whether the trait is negative or positive. At some point in my life, I was overweight and didn't do anything about it. Whenever someone would make a comment to me, I would reply, 'it is a sign of good living'. It was not until I had to loose weight due to a medical condition did I accept it was a sign of bad living. You can not change your character until you accept that you need to change, it takes a paradigm shift in your thinking pattern to realise that change is necessary, before it becomes an emergency.

If you are really serious about developing yourself and finding who you are, you need to take a good look at the things you do that build your character. Your daily behaviours and habits, are they good? Are they positive? Do they add value? Are you a player or are you a spectator? Do you wait for things to happen or do you initiate things to happen? These are some key questions to ask yourself when judging your character, if you have positive answers to these question, good, then you can maintain what you are doing that is right. But, if you have negative answers from this evaluation, you need to draw up a plan of action to transform your character and work on it.

So how do we build our character to become positive? How do we transform a negative character into a positive transformed character? The secrets to the transformation of character is doing the right things at the right time, whether somebody is watching you or not and doing them all the time. Its called, 'performing for the audience of one'.

Changing Your Character

Whether you are old or young, you can develop new character traits and transform the way you live your life. Most people see themselves in a positive light and try to put a positive spin on a bad character trait. However the truth is, what is bad can only stay bad unless it is changed. Your personal character traits are the attitudes you tend to exhibit when dealing with challenges and tasks. Before you decide to change these attitudes you need to be motivated by a desire. At some point in my life, I had the desire to bring some order into my life because, I was just living without any direction or any focus; this desire caused me to create myself a plan for my life, more like a blueprint to my purpose and since I did that I have never looked back.

To change your character you need to take a proactive approach, you need to take responsibility for who you are, what you are; you need to know why you do what you do. Then you will be able to set the wheels of progress in motion. Being proactive requires you to decide for yourself how you want to be and not let your circumstances decide or dictate for you. So when you want a promotion at work, you do not wait for it to come to you, you create the atmosphere to make it happen for you. You set your target on how you are going to achieve the goal of the promotion and you make it happen, you become the indispensable employee, you be the first to get to work and you become the last to leave work. You become the employee that always goes the extra mile; then and only then will you be able to command the promotion that you desire. This example can apply to any goal you desire to follow. When you are building a character trait, you are always performing for the audience of one, but believe me someone else is always watching.

Always keep The End In Mind

The best way to build a positive and sound character is to focus on your ultimate goal in life. When you have something to look forward to, you have a reason to continue going. When I had the revelation of these truths in my life, I wrote down my manifesto, my guiding rules and principles. I have altered them a few times but the whole basis is still there. You have to start by laying out your life and view it from the outside looking in, so when you have departed the earth, the earth will know that you showed up and contributed. Your generation will have had the benefit of your presence and contribution.

There have been so many people that have shown up and left and nothing was said of them, however, there are a few that have left a footprint behind. The likes of Dr. Martin Luther King Jr., Thomas A. Edison, Albert Einstein, Abraham Lincoln, Ralph Waldo Emerson, Michelangelo, Leonardo Da Vinci. These names are real people that were celebrated because of their character, their attitude and the impact they made in their generation. They made it a point to follow their destiny, they set goals for themselves and targets. They decided not yield to what their environment was telling them or what their peers or even their parents were telling them. They stood firm in the face of adversity and would not let the obstacles and distractions of life pull them down. That's why we can celebrate them today. They were part of that five percent of their generation that were successful while the other ninety five percent were just getting by.

What changes do you need to make in your life plan? What do you need to write into your life plan that is not there right now?

Daily Management

The management of your plan is essential to building your character. You don't just write a plan, you also execute it, otherwise the whole process is defeated.

Henry Ford said;

'Life is a series of experiences, each one of which makes us bigger, even though sometimes it is hard to realise this; for the world was built to develop character and we must learn that the setbacks and grieves, which we endure, help us in our marching onward'

I don't think it could be put any better; what we do everyday and how we do it, will determine our strength of character, and how successful we become. We are bound to face challenges and obstacles but it is the experiences that we have been through, the little successes we have experienced along the way that will take us to that higher place.

Henry Ford had so many setbacks before he finally made the breakthrough he was looking for. Also, remember Thomas A. Edison failed ten thousand times before his success, yet he was doing what he was always doing, managing his life daily with the end product in mind.

In life, we only have the opportunity to manage today, yesterday is gone, you can not add to it neither can you subtract from it, that is why you have to make today count because your tomorrow will become your today and whatever you do today becomes you.

It is important to correctly manage you time to effectively navigate through the path that you take in life, key questions to ask yourself are:

- For me to accomplish this task, what is required of me?
- For me to accomplish this task, what is the return for me?
- For me to accomplish this task, what is the reward for me?

You need a positive character to be able to stand when all is lost, when you need to start over, when you need to make tough decisions, and when people depend on you to make the right call. There are various traits to a positive character. A person that has a positive character will demonstrate some of the following behaviour and habitual traits:

Trustworthiness: The attributes of a trustworthy character are honesty, loyalty, and reliability. Your word is your bond, you are known to stick to whatever you say. You do the right thing, and you don't deceive, cheat, or steal. That's what trustworthiness is.

Respect: Being respectful of others means to be considerate of the views, opinions and attitudes of others and to be tolerant of their differences in opinion whether you agree or not. It also means to be good mannered. Your decisions are made based on the respect you show to your health and the health of others. You treat people and property with care.

Responsibility: You take responsibility for your actions, you exercise self-control, you think before you act and consider the consequences. People that exhibit these traits are accountable for their choices and decisions, they don't blame others for their actions. Responsible people try to do their best, and they persevere even when things don't go as planned.

Fairness: Fair people play by the rules, they wait for their turn in any task before them and share. They are open-minded, and listen to others. They never take advantage of others, and don't assign blame to others.

Caring: Caring about other people and being compassionate towards others is another positive character trait. When you show care toward others, you make them feel good about themselves. A caring person is also seen to continuously express gratitude. You have a forgiving heart, and you are always on hand to help people in need.

Benefits of a Positive Character

The attitude you take into a task is most definitely going to determine the outcome of it. If you go into a task with a defeated attitude, you are most likely going to fail at the end of the task or give up at the first sign of difficulty.

However, if you go into a task with the belief that nothing is going to stop you from achieving success, you are on the right path to achieving the goal you set for yourself. When Henry Ford was building his Model T car for mass production, he failed on some occasions, but he stuck to the task and eventually came up with the model T that revolutionised the use of the automobile in the nineteenth century. Outstanding inventors and successful leaders have left different legacies that we see today because of their positive character and attitude towards life. They did not see defeat as the ultimate, they saw defeat as a setback that could be overcome through sheer determination.

A positive attitude towards other people opens doors of favour and warmth back to you. If you help someone, when you need help, you will get help from someone else. It's the law of sowing and reaping, it's also part of the law of return and the law of cause and effect. When you help someone you are in a win-win situation because, you are helping yourself to fulfilling part of you existence, and also you are helping someone else do the same.

Key Learning Points

1. Your character is built from your daily habits.
2. There are positive character traits and there are negative traits.
3. You can change you character.
4. A positive character can yield success in life, while a negative character can result in failure.

Chapter 5

Your Values And Belief System

'Make Your Life Decisions Early and Manage Them Daily'

What do you believe?

You believe yourself into who you become in life. We all have dreams and ambitions, things we want to achieve, some of us achieve them while some of us don't, we go around the wheel of life, with somebody else turning the wheel. There were two heavyweight boxers, one said I am the greatest and the other said I am out of control. He that said he was the greatest was eventually voted to be the sports personality of the century, the other became out of control and went to prison.

Your beliefs are what you speak out and become you, if you believe in positive words and speak them out, positive things will happen to you, however if you believe in negative words and say them, that will become your reality.

Every human being has a belief, the question is, are you believing in positively or are you believing in negativity? Every human being dreams and has thoughts and desires, most of the time, these thoughts are positive. The fact that you have these thoughts is an indication and a fact that it is possible that you can achieve these thoughts. If you could not achieve your thoughts, the thoughts will not even come to you. You are a creative being and that is why you can dream and dream big. Your belief system is the bedrock of everything in your life, it is what you believe that you act out into a behaviour. It is this behaviour that becomes a habit in you, this habit becomes your character and attitude which then forms your reputation which you are judged by.

Our values give birth to our beliefs, it is what provides the means of that which is important to us. These are the ideals we live our lives by, the rules that guide us in the decisions we make that affect our lives. Having values that create a positive view of your life will allow you to open your mind to possibilities and push you to take chances in life. It will give you the kind of energy to think yourself out of what seems to be an impossible situation.

What is your Value System?

Your value system determines the kind of beliefs you exhibit, it is the policy maker of your being, your existence and your reality. It is your value system that holds the significance and meaning to your existence. It's your values that give meaning to the life that you live, it influences the daily decisions you make and the actions you take. Understanding and identifying with your value system will enable you to create your beliefs and reality. Every human being has various values and these values make up your value system which form your belief system.

You exhibit various values that require different levels of priority; your values show up in your behaviour depending on what mood you find yourself. It is good practice to identify which are the values you place priority on. Your values need to be organised so as to build your belief system in a positive way. Our values are exhibited in different ways depending on the situation. Whether you are in a peaceful or in a conflicting environment, you tend to exhibit different values to deal with the situation you find yourself in and it is at this point that you have a clear view of what values are dear to you. It is these values that eventually form your belief system which becomes the basis of your character.

Your Belief System

Who you are and what you become is based on your belief system. Your reality came from what you believed. Your belief system was developed through your associations over the period of your development which includes; your parents, your peers, your friends and your environment. As you grow up, depending on the environment, there may be a tendency for you to develop a fear of doing certain things. There is an in-built fear that develops over a period of time that boxes up our possibilities and ambitions. This fear prohibits our inner desires to come out and be realised and this brings about limiting beliefs. This is why you decide to settle for an average life, a life that does not stretch beyond its comfort zone. When you struggle with limiting beliefs, you will always live within your means, never engage in the possibility of taking risks.

Origin of Limiting Beliefs

When you are born into the world you are new, then you grow up. As a kid in this world, you are open to try anything, you have a fearless attitude to life. You come with a belief of asking for things and getting them, a belief of all things are possible. This was the kind of belief the Apostle

Chapter 5

Peter had when the Bible said he walked on water. Have you noticed a child, they seem to want to try everything. If you leave a child and just observe, the child will gravitate to anything they see, whether it is fire, water, or light. The only thing I have not seen a child gravitate towards is darkness, I might be wrong, but I have not seen it; this goes to show the positive embedded belief that the baby came into the world with.

Over years of growing up the original beliefs we had as children become conditioned and limits are placed on our ability to believe for the impossible. Because of our environment, such as neighbourhoods we grew up in, families we grew up with, parents and relatives we listened to, we often succumb to the trappings of our surroundings.

As a kid in Africa, I grew up in a neighbourhood where the type of properties were buildings with blocks of four flats. These were the type of buildings around the area at that time. Because these were the properties I saw and lived in, my mind was conditioned to think these kind of buildings were the norm. I use to think a detached three or four bedroom house was not normal; this is a classic example on how the environment you grow up in can shape your beliefs into a box.

Another way in which your beliefs can be limited is through your parents telling you things that place a limit on your creativity or your achievement. An example is when you want to try out a vocational activity such as a sport or drama; they might tell you 'why are you wasting your time, you are not good at it anyway'. When you hear that over and over, you tend to build a limiting belief that hampers you from trying new things because you have built up a belief of failure due to what you were told when you were young.

Events or history can cast doubts over our belief system. A belief of *cheating to succeed* is exhibited from seeing people achieve short term success through bending the rules. For example; taking advantage of being in a position of responsibility, but not being responsible, or believing that, unless you cheat your way through life success is not attainable. So based on that belief, you build the tendency of taking shortcuts in going about your different tasks and end up with the possibility of achieving nothing or getting into trouble because of the belief system you decided to follow.

The origin of all these limitations stem from FEAR:

Fear of the unknown,

Fear of failure,

Fear of what people might say,

Fear of going higher,

Fear of leaving your comfort zone.

There are so many things that put fear in our hearts. It is mainly due to the fact that in our development we have witnessed people living average lives, placing themselves in boxes of containment, while refusing to try the unknown. Because they have not tried it, they believe in extending their experiences to you and advise you to follow their footpath of just enough and average.

What is Fear?

The definition of fear is explained in different terms, but the basic view of fear is; to feel a painful apprehension of something; to be afraid of something; to consider or expect with emotion or solicitude.

Types of Fear

The use of the word fear varies depending on the context. We experience fear in our lives through reactions to a circumstance, such as the possibility of an imminent attack from a deadly animal, or being in a dangerous environment. We also experience another type of fear which comes from our inner self due to different stimuli. Fear is either Instinctive or Psychological.

Instinctive Fear

Instinctive fear is the type of fear that is associated with the occurrence of imminent danger, possibly from attack or the possibility of attack, being in a scary environment.

Instinctive fear comes upon us when we experience an event that is scary, such as an attack of some kind. When we are in a scary location, an example can be walking in a graveyard at about midnight; that can be a scary experience for a lot of people. Or a young lady walking home in the evening from the movies and sees a group of four noisy young men walking towards her, might experience the fear of being attacked.

… Chapter 5

Psychological Fear

Psychological fear deals with the subconscious programmes that our mind works with. It is the fear of the unknown; it is the fear that stops us from achieving, it is the fear that keeps us in the comfort zones of our lives. It is the fear that feeds our belief system, it is the fear that promotes the idea that 'being average is okay'. When you operate with this kind of fear, you hardly ever take chances, you always play it safe. This fear can propel us forward or hold us back. If we let fear keep us in a box and stop us from making a decision to move forward, we will end up stagnated. However, it is this fear that can propel you to greater heights in life.

The Seven Psychological Fears

These are the basic fears that people need to look out for during their development and the duration of their life:

1. **Fear of Poverty:** This fear is embedded in the mind through the associations and the environment you grow up in. It affects your decision making. In order for you to conquer this fear, you need to be success conscious, you need to get over the idea that you are limited because it is you that is placing that block

on your mind. You need to fill your mind with the emotion of success.

2. **Fear of Criticism:** I have come to the understanding that some people decide not to ask questions for different reasons. A group of people don't ask because they know the answer, another group because of pride, and the final group because of fear. The ones that do not ask because of fear, simply do not want to be criticised and do not want to be seen as being stupid or dumb. But I have come to the realisation that the real dumb people are those who don't ask and don't even know the answer. The smart people are the ones that ask questions, they seek knowledge, they seek information, they want to grow and develop themselves.

3. **Fear of What 'THEY' Will 'Say':** There are a group of people called 'they', a lot of people talk about them but nobody really knows who 'they' are. These people are in the minds of some people, they destroy the imagination of people with dreams, cut down people's initiative. They are as powerful as you allow them to be. You should not give anybody power to stop you from being you.

4. **Fear of Sickness:** The fear of falling ill and being ridden with disease which hampers ones ability to think beyond the limitations of the mind. This fear results in imaginary illness and strikes you down at your prime, the time when you should be operating at your most productive period in life.

5. **Fear of Loosing Love:** This fear results and is expressed in the form of jealousy. It is a destructive venom and a motivating force that can stop people from making the right call on their life.

6. **Fear of Old Age:** Men and women harbour the fear of growing old. However, it is at a mature age that some of the major breakthroughs in business success have occurred. Colonel Saunders of the KFC Chicken brand made his business breakthrough at the age of sixty five. It has been in mature years that major leaders developed the wisdom of living a life of legacy building, the likes of Bill Clinton former United States President, Jimmy Carter, Nelson Mandela, and the list goes on.

7. **Fear of Death:** The biggest fear that has hampered the progress of a lot of people and has stopped a lot of people from taking major strides in life is the fear of death.

These fears need to be eliminated from your mind so as to be able to conquer the limiting beliefs that have been formed in your mind.

Overcoming Fear

Before we can overcome the fear we have built up over the years, we need to accept some necessary truths at the beginning of the process.

You Have the Guarantee of a Successful Life: You are guaranteed success if you accept your purpose in life and walk in it. You need to understand that only you can limit your success.

There are no Mistakes in Life: In everyday life decisions are made that affect our actions and in turn our lives. All decisions made are the right ones at the time that they were made; and only you will know that a decision made was wrong if you believe it to be so. A decision you make leads you to another level of decision making. Your life is a journey of development, trials, tribulations, and tests, and every decision you make is part of the tests that you go through to get to your destination.

Make That Decision Anyway: More often than not, we fear to make decisions because we think it might be the wrong one. Sometimes to allay the fear, the best thing to do is make the decision anyway, because you can make another stride in your path of life instead of staying in the same position due to the lack of a decision.

Let Go of Your Fear By Asking 'What if': When the fear comes that tries to limit you advancement in any way, ask yourself, what if you do make the decision and it happens to be the right one? Question the fear that comes into your mind, challenge it's validity. Fear will always question your validity and character; turn the tables around. To overcome this fear, give it a taste of it's own medicine, question it's validity in your mind.

Trust in Your Character and Identity: You need to believe in yourself and your identity, know who you are. The first thing fear attacks is your identity, which is your mind. Everything about you comes from your mind. That is why your brain is charged with so many functions, it is the epicentre of all functions in your body. It is the control centre that guides you, that room of operation, it does trillions of calculations on your behalf daily. You need to cultivate it, by feeding it with the right and correct information.

Weigh up All the Available Options: All options to a fear need to be weighed up. Is it necessary to harbour this fear? The thought, is it really true? Remember you make your future through your thoughts.

Weigh up All the Pros and Cons from the Options: Weigh up all the advantages and disadvantages of each option available to you. With this you get a better view of the option or decision you have decided to take.

Replace The Vacuum that Fear has Left Behind: If a space is left vacant, what was taken from there will come back seven times stronger when the vacuum is still there, It is important to replace the space created by the removal of fear with its opposite, positive thoughts, the 'I can do' thoughts, the 'I believe thoughts'. Replace the fear with Faith, faith in your abilities, faith in yourself, faith that 'whatever you do will be successful' So, what is faith?

Faith

What is Faith?

Faith is the starting point of all achievement, faith is what transforms the natural into supernatural. Faith transforms ordinary thoughts by a man into reality. Faith is the basis of all miracles that can not be explained by science.

You need to work on your mind in order to build up your faith, through positive thoughts and positive desires. In the areas of your mind that have been built up with negative habits, you need to build the faith that will change these habits and attitudes. The information you feed your mind will build your future, feeding your mind with the new found faith will help transform you.

The law of Auto-suggestion is the key to building your faith. Repeatedly suggesting success into your mind is a repetitive reminder of who you are. You have to think your way into your possibilities, as well as be able to think your way out of difficult situations.

Love plays an important part in the building of faith. All the people that have operated in true faith, have operated in love. Take Mahatmha Ghandhi for instance, because of his love for people, he mobilised over two hundred million people to peacefully demonstrate against the tyranny of the class system in India. Mother Theresa, because of her love for children, her faith allowed her to galvanise people around the world to recognise her as one of the most influential people around the world through her orphanage. Bill Gates, through his faith and love for people, produced software that has made it easy for people to use computers all around the world today and still influence the world continuously through his foundation. Nelson Mandela, because of the love he had for his people, he had faith that one day he would be a free man and would rule his country out of its darkest days. Jesus Christ, because of his love that he had for the world, gave up his life and had the faith that his sacrifice would not be for nothing, that he would rise up and his followers would come back to the fellowship of God the father.

Faith plays a big part in the way we live. It takes faith to go to bed and believe you will wake up in the morning. However, we limit our faith due to fears that we allow to linger around us. Faith removes limitations from our thoughts, we need to exercise our faith to get us out of our average living.

Building Your faith

One of the most significant and successful ways to build faith is through the principle of Auto-suggestion. It is a fact that, a man is what he declares himself to be. If you continue to declare yourself to be a looser, you eventually become a looser. It is easy for the mind to attract negative stimuli because it does not take much effort for the attraction of negative stimuli. However, on the other hand, to attract positive stimuli, the mind has to be conditioned to attract positive stimuli that is attractive to positive attributes and the natural law process.

Auto-suggestion works both in a negative way and a positive way After the programming of the receptors of your brain to accept positive stimuli, only then, can your mind programme and translate the positive information that it is receiving. It all depends on your state of mind for you to achieve anything, listen to Kristone the poet;

'If You Think You're Beaten'

'If you think you're beaten, you are, If you think you dare not, you don't. If you'd like to win, but think you can't, It's almost for sure, you won't.

If you think you're losing, you've lost. For out in the world we find - Success begins with a person's will, It's all in the state of mind.

If you think you're outclassed, you are, You've got to think high to rise. You have to stay with it, In order to win the prize.

Life's battles don't always go, to the one with the better plan. For more often than not, you will win, If only you think you can.'

Whatever you programme into your mind is what will be delivered to you as a reality.

Key Learning Points

1. You are who you say you are.
2. Your beliefs come from your associations and your environment.
3. You learn your beliefs, so that means you can change them.
4. Fear can be conquered.
5. Faith is the opposite of fear.

Chapter 6

The Road Map To Transformation

'What is in Your Hand is most certainly a Link to Your Future'

The great Martin Luther King Jr.'s most famous words, 'I have a Dream', continue to ring all around the world. However, Dr. King's famous words were not synonymous to him alone, everyone has a dream. The problem is most people are so timid and too scared to even entertain their dream in their mind for even a few seconds. Someone or something has helped programme their minds to limit them to what they see as their current circumstance.

For any dreams you might harbour in your heart, you need a desire that is so strong, that you will give anything and everything to achieve it.

After the transformation of your behaviours, habits, character, attitude, values and your belief system; now you are ready to go on a journey of locating your footpath to your future. It's now time to find out why you were born. Now you can start your Mona Lisa, your own masterpiece.

The first step to your journey is finding out what you are passionate about. There are so many ways or guidelines to help identify the reason for your existence. Find the things that you love doing, things that you are passionate about.

What Problems Stare You In The Face?

You were placed on this earth to correct a defect, to solve a problem that requires a solution. What problems surround you that keep cropping up? Pay close attention to those things that irritate you, this is a clue to your existence. You were not placed on the earth to live an average life, a life of not contributing to the development of your generation.

Over the years, the world has gone through so much development. These breakthroughs have taken place because of people just like you and me. Be it in the development of energy resources, automobiles, hospitality, or technology; these developments have all been made possible by people that have decided to find the true meaning to their existence. Every person on this earth is a problem solver and the reason why there are so many problems is because people have not connected with their inner self to find out their reason for existence. It is the problem that you see, that will bring out the creativity within you to solve it. Science has proven that everyone born has his or her own unique DNA, that means, we all have our own unique identity. Furthermore; that means, only one person can do something that is specific to that person. Breaking this down, in a puzzle, a piece can only fit into its designated position; so that means, we all have a role in making the world a better place. Simply put because we are not all doing what we have been called to do, that is why the earth is the way it is.

Everybody that was sent into this earth at some point, was called for; Edison for the electric bulb, the Wright brothers for the aeroplane, Sir Isaac Newton for the developments in Science and Physics, Bill Gates for the development of user-friendly Computer Software, Willis Carrier, the inventor of the first air conditioner; and the list goes on and on.

There have been so many breakthroughs in science that have come from the creativity of people, who stepped up to the stage and took their place in history. Those who made their existence count for good and greatness, all because they solved a problem. What problems are before you? These are an inclination to your existence on earth.

What Do You Love Doing?

What is that thing that you love doing so much that, you can spend hours and hours at it and not think you have spent a minute? You were endowed with various gifts when you were sent into the earth. Through the ages, men and women have come into the world and deposited what was in their heart, some are still alive while some have departed. These people that poured themselves out to the world were rewarded both in life and in death. Princess Diana had such compassion and love for the needy, she gained favour from nearly all the leaders and influential people around the world. Bill Gates had a love for computers and software, this led him to abandon his first degree in law to start work on designing software with his then business partner. Now he is celebrated for the creation of Microsoft, the company that gave us Windows software that transformed the use of computers in the 80's and 90's on into the 21st century. Thomas Edison loved making things, that's why he spent so much time working on the creation of the electric light bulb. As previously mentioned he failed ten thousand times and even with that he was driven by this passion to make things work, he loved to help people. Henry Ford, with his Model T automobile; despite his failures, Henry was persistent in his manufacture of the mass production of the Model T, which transformed the ownership of cheap affordable automobiles to the mass public. Again, he loved to create and he loved to help people.

The above names mentioned all demonstrated a love for what they do or did, a love for people and a love to serve people. Love plays a very important part in walking the footpath to a fulfilled life.

Love is such a powerful force that it is the master of all emotions. It is the one emotion that can not be matched in power. True love conquers all things. The love of your creator causes Him to reveal the secret things in your heart that will show you the way to go in your footpath of life.

Love drives passion and persistence, it gives you a power to do the unthinkable, the unbelievable. When you love something you become an expert on that thing, you take a keen interest in that thing, you educate yourself about that thing.

You could love watching films, and know everything about the way they are made. From different directors, and their styles, to their methods of story telling; this may very well lead you into working in the film production industry.

The love of something drives you to do everything to protect its image. If you love doing something over and over again and would do it happily even if you were not paid to do it, that is a clue to what you are supposed to be doing in life.

In the time of old, Moses, the leader that led the Israelites out of Egypt, did not like nor did he tolerate injustice. This was a trait in him that led him to finally accept his assignment of leadership of the Jews out of Egypt through the Red Sea.

King David, before he was king, another man that hated injustice, went up against the giant Goliath that was terrorising the Jews.

My father had a love for educating people. Even though he did not study teaching or education as a primary vocation and career, he reverted back to teaching and educating the younger generation.

Your assignment in life is strongly associated with what you love and how it affects the people around you.

What Do You Hate?

What do you get angry about? What is that thing that infuriates you that you just want to fix? Before I realised my purpose in life I would get so angry when I saw young people behaving badly, without any discipline or focus, it use to really get under my skin. Then God showed me how to encourage them, organise events for them and how to guide them along their path in the decisions they made. What I am trying to say here is; because of the anger I had towards the indiscipline and their lack of focus, I saw that I had a responsibility in guiding the young generation in fulfilling their destiny.

Moses the deliverer of Israel hated slavery, as shown when he killed an Egyptian soldier for beating up an Israelite slave. Mother Theresa hated seeing children suffer, so she started her orphanage to take in children that had no where to go. Nelson Mandela hated injustice against his people, so he led a campaign against the apartheid regime in South Africa, which culminated in him going to prison for it and eventually returning as the President of his country.

Your anger needs to be focused, measured and deliberate. If your anger is not controlled it can yield the wrong results for you. Lets take another look at the leader of the people of Israel, Moses, who led them into the wilderness. On occasion he got angry due to the behaviour traits of his followers. This anger caused him to loose his temper and disobey a simple instruction from God to speak to the rock, but instead Moses hit the rock with his staff. The repercussion was that Moses was forbidden to enter the promised land. Imagine something you have been working for and in a split second lose it through anger, a lack of self-control and a lack of following instructions. The hate I am talking about here is a passion against what you do not like and can not tolerate. This type of anger is measured and focused in achieving a settlement of what the problem is.

The history of the modern day civil rights movement was rooted in the early 1960s, but the true movement started way back in the United States on December 1, 1955. This was the day when an unknown seamstress in Montgomery, Alabama refused to give up her bus seat to a white passenger. This brave woman, was arrested and fined for violating a city ordinance, but her lonely act of defiance began a movement that ended legal segregation in America, and made her an inspiration to freedom-loving people everywhere. Here is her story:

It was a cold winter evening in 1955, she boarded a bus and sat down on an aisle seat. After the bus had travelled three stops, a group of passengers boarded, with the seats full and a man standing, the driver asked her to stand up so the man could sit down, she refused. She did not like the injustice, discrimination, or the segregation that had long been going on. She decided that day in her heart that enough is enough. She said within herself, 'I am not standing for this anymore'. The bus driver refused to move the bus, he said if she did not get up, he would have her arrested, she said he should go ahead. He stopped the bus some people came off the bus. After a while two policemen turned up and asked her, was she told to stand up for the man to sit and she refused? She answered yes, he asked, why did she not stand up? and she replied, she does not think she should have to stand up and then she asked him,

'Why did they push us around?'

And he said, and she quotes him,

"I don't know, but the law is the law and you are under arrest."

She said, in an interview,

'But I made up my mind that I would not give in any longer to legally-imposed racial segregation and of course my arrest brought about protests for more than a year'.

In future interviews she said and I quote, 'I was arrested on a Thursday evening, and on Friday evening is when they had the meeting at the Dexter Avenue Baptist Church, where Dr. Martin Luther King was the pastor. A number of citizens came and I told them the story and from then on, it became news about my being arrested. My trial was December 5th, when they found me guilty. The lawyers Fred Gray and Charles Langford, who represented me, filed an appeal and, of course, I didn't pay any fine. We set a meeting at the Holt Street Baptist Church on the evening of December 5th, because December 5th was the day the people stayed off in large numbers and did not ride the bus. In fact, most of the buses, I think all of them were just about empty with the exception of maybe very, very few people. When they found out that one day's protest had kept people off the bus, it came to a vote and unanimously, it was decided that they would not ride the buses anymore until changes for the better were made.

As I look back on those days, it's just like a dream. The only thing that bothered me was that we waited so long to make this protest and to let it be known wherever we go that all of us should be free and equal and have all opportunities that others should have.'

It was this event that led to the civil rights movement that we read about in our history books and on the internet today. And who was this great woman? None other than Rosa Parks. She had an anger against the treatment she and her people were receiving from the then dominant white supremacist. She sat down for what she believed in, and the ripple effect ignited a fire that culminated in a dream that Martin Luther King Jr., had that was fulfilled in Barack

Obama moving into the White House as President of the United States.

For you to achieve anything of significance, you need to have a burning desire, a yearning, and a dislike for mediocrity. Understand this, whatever you tolerate becomes acceptable to you and you lose the ability to change it. What is that thing that you hate that you have a passion to change? I reiterate; that is a clue and a key to your existence on earth.

What Brings Tears To Your Eyes?

When you feel the pain of others and empathise with them, when you have a heart of compassion for a situation that others are having a bad experience from, this is an indication of something you are suppose to fix. Sickness, disease, ignorance, abuse, poverty and corruption are all ills in society that need fixing. A compassionate person will see the ills as if they themselves are the person experiencing them, in order to be a source of healing.

To fix a problem requires knowledge, wisdom and influence. No one will listen to a carpenter telling everyone that he can perform brain surgery or a chef saying he can fly a spaceship to the moon. That's why everyone that is suppose to be the healer to an ill situation needs to have knowledge of the situation or problem he or she is dealing with. Your compassion is a driving force in the problem you are meant to solve.

María Eva Duarte de Perón; born 7 May 1919 was the second wife of Juan Peron, the President of Argentina between 1945 – 1955 and 1973 – 1974. Maria served as the First Lady of Argentina from 1946 until her death in 1952. She is often referred to as simply Eva Perón, or by the affectionate name Evita, which literally translates into English as 'Little Eva'.

The fourth of five children, she was born out of wedlock in the village of Los Toldos in rural Argentina. In 1934, at the age of 15, she went to the nation's capital of Buenos Aires, where she pursued a career as a stage, radio, and film actress. She met Colonel Juan Peron on January 22, 1944, in Buenos Aires during a charity event at the Luna Park Stadium to benefit the victims of an earthquake in San Juan, Argentina. The two were married the following year. In 1946, Juan Perón was elected President of Argentina. Over the course of the next six years, Eva Perón became powerful within the Pro-Peronist trade unions, essentially for speaking on behalf of the labour rights movement. She was also in charge of the Ministries of Labour and Health, founded and ran the charitable Eva Peron Foundation, championed woman suffrage in Argentina, and founded and ran the nation's first large-scale female political party, the Female Peronist Party.

Over the years the Eva Peron Foundation grew and within a few years, the foundation had assets in cash and goods in excess of three billion pesos, or over $200 million at the exchange rate of the late 1940s. It employed about 14,000 workers, of which 6,000 were construction workers, and 26 priests. It purchased and distributed annually 400,000 pairs of shoes, 500,000 sewing machines, and 200,000 cooking pots. The foundation also gave scholarships, built homes, hospitals, and other charitable institutions. Every aspect of the foundation was under Evita's supervision. The foundation also built entire communities, such as Evita City, which still exists today. Fraser and Navarro her biographers, claim, that due to the works and health services of the foundation, for the first time in history there was no inequality in Argentine's health care.

Fraser and Navarro write that it was Evita's work with the foundation that played a large role in her idealization,

Evita set aside many hours per day to meet with the poor who requested help from her foundation. During these meetings with the poor, Evita often kissed the poor and allowed them to kiss her. Evita was even witnessed placing her hands in the suppurated wounds of the sick and poor, touching those blighted with leprosy.

Fraser and Navarro also write that toward the end of her life, Evita was working as many as 20 and 22 hours per day in her foundation, often ignoring her husband's request that she cut back on her workload and take the weekends off. The more she worked with the poor in her foundation, the more she adopted an outraged attitude toward the existence of poverty, saying,

"Sometimes I have wished my insults were slaps or lashes. I've wanted to hit people in the face to make them see, if only for a day, what I see each day I help the people."

These are the words of someone that had an overwhelming compassion to the needy. Crassweller another biographer, also writes in his biography of Evita, that she became fanatical about her work in the foundation and felt on a crusade against the very concept and existence of poverty and social ills.

Apart from being a passionate woman that despised poverty, she was a political icon that travelled the world representing her country on the European Rainbow Tour. As a political leader she formed the first women's political party in Argentina's history, the Female Peronist Party. She was an inspirational servant leader to her people and despite suffering from ill health due to cancer, she still attended public functions after pumping herself with painkillers before and after attending every event. This is from a girl that was born out of wedlock, grew up in poverty after her father left her mother, she rose to become the leader of a nation. Even though she was not the official Argentine president, she was the peoples president, she had the people in her heart and the people had her in theirs. However, she could not beat her illness of cancer and it got the best of her in 1952 and she died at the early age of 33, but she accomplished her reason for existence despite her beginnings and also her early end.

What is it that you can not stand, that makes you want to cry and wish you could fix? Believe me, you can fix it,

Chapter 6

Rome was not built in a day, it took builders to lay it brick by brick. There is a Chinese proverb that goes;

The journey of a thousand miles begins with one step'.

Why don't you take that step today and begin your thousand mile journey to success.

The Decisions You Make Will Determine How Quick It Takes

It is very easy to take the wrong direction in life and wonder in the wilderness going round in circles. Finding direction is very important and connecting with wisdom early on in life is equally important and key to building a successful life.

Before I go any further, let me be clear right now; whatever or whoever you believe in, as far as I am concerned, I believe that we as a human race did not just come into existence through evolution, we were created by a creator. You can determine within yourself who or what you want to believe, however, when all is said and done, the creator will reveal himself to his created when he is good and ready.

I have come to realise that, if your creator really wants to use you to achieve something, He does not leave you alone until you do that which he wants you to do.

There are three people that I will give as an example, two dead and one living.

Jonah was a prophet in the Holy Bible, sent to warn the people of Nineveh about their behaviour. But because of his dislike of the people and wanting to be their judge and executioner, he thought in his wisdom that he would not go and warn them and would rather they suffer the wrath of God. Jonah decided to go on a boat ride to Tarshish, he thought in his mind that he could get away from the creator.

I am just going to stop here for a minute, imagine the created thinking he can hide from the creator amongst other created. Your creator created everything, including space, you can not get away from him, so there is no point in trying.

Well, back to Jonah. So he got on the boat enjoying the initial view, he did not know the creator was watching. Then the creator sneezed, and it brought Jonah back to his senses. This sneeze created a storm that was causing distress to the boat and also brought Jonah back to his sense of responsibility. Jonah asked to be thrown overboard and he was, but the creator is one that gives second, third and even fourth chances; a big whale was provided as a safety net for the repented Jonah to retrace his character and fix his attitude. It was like putting iron into fire to get rid of all the dirt and blemish. The story concluded with Jonah going to do what he was told and the people of Nineveh repenting and turning their ways back to God.

Another great leader was King David, the only person to be referenced as a man after God's own heart. King David lost his focus when he decided to wonder to the window of his palace instead of focusing on the vision of leading the nation of Israel. It was the diversion to the window that caused him to see a naked woman bathing, a naked woman by the name of Bathsheba who had a husband that was serving in King David's army. Well, King David had an affair with Bathsheba and orchestrated a plan for Uriah to be killed in battle. Well, that led to a lot of turmoil in the palace of the King. He brought Bathsheba into his family and the baby from the initial affair died. his punishment from God was that turmoil would not leave his household and war would not leave his kingdom as king. his own son attempted to kill him and the temple that he wanted to build for God, he was not allowed because of his tainted hands.

When you are distracted from following your vision, punishment comes upon the people around you and those that you are associated with. In today's terms, we can call it collateral damage. King David lost his first son from Bathsheba and he lost his other son Absalom. There was so much strife in his household.

The last person is me. My creator laid a path for me when I was young. However, I continually diverted from it, choosing instead to do what was pleasing to me. I worked on jobs I did not like just to pay bills and live an average life. Yet I continued to ask God for my direction in life. I tried different ventures, but they did not come off. I continued to plunge money into other ideas, however, I harboured the belief and faith that God would reveal Himself and my purpose to me. I continued working on a job I did not like, getting a salary that always just covered my bills and some, but I never experienced satisfaction. Even my faith in the church was wearing thin. Let me be clear, when I say church, I mean the body of Christ as I am a Christian. At that point in my life there were one or two things that kept me going, my faith in God, my character and I believe my mother's prayers over me. I was a team leader in my church, but I had to take time out because of hurt and also because I felt God was leading me in a different direction. Little did I know that everything that I needed to find who I was and what I was supposed to do and where I am to learn, was right where I was. However, in my ignorance, I focused on trying to work to raise money for my business ventures, which I believed was my next calling, and would you believe it, my employment was terminated.

I say here, beware of what you ask God for, because, you will definitely get it. So, with no job, and a lot of time on my hands, God took me through a process of refining the second time in my life. That's why I said, God is a creator that will give you chance after chance after chance. Next I focused on building a new career. I started a business that I went back to university to study for, but it was proving difficult as well as extremely expensive. I made a commitment that year that this was it; yet as the target and goals I set for myself were getting closer, I was getting more agitated. In spite of my frustrations I have always remembered this one message my Pastor and other men of the Christian faith have preached; *'What skill you have that you enjoy doing, is a key to your destiny'*. So I spent that month of June, which was a special month on the calendar of our church, to pray and fast myself completely to the thought that this is going to make or break me. I have gone through different teachings, motivational tapes, leadership and self-development books so I knew all the lingo and principles, now I wanted action. So, as I was talking to friends and listening and thinking also, one skill in particular kept coming up. In everything, be it location, employment, in the business, that skill was always showing itself. So I decided to look for professional advice about this skill. I got the opportunity to go to a seminar to find out about more about this skill, but before I got the opportunity to attend that seminar, another opportunity came my way, which was a shadow of the seminar that I was going to attend initially. It is funny, because this other workshop opportunity was there as a distraction from what I was suppose to be doing. The counterfeit opportunity that came my way was round the corner from my house, all I needed to do was just drive for about twenty five minutes and go through an hour long presentation and done. As

Chapter 6

eager as I was to attend the briefing, when the day came, I just could not go, I simply stayed at home. On the other hand the initial seminar, which was a two-day seminar, was up in London and I lived in Kent. It was going to cost me about forty pounds for travel for the two days, yet I was geared up for it and prepared myself. On the day of the seminar, I got a lift to the train station by my wife, I bought my ticket, waited in the car with her for the train to come. We talked about what we were going to do in the time of change that was happening around us. Finally, we bid our goodbyes and I went down the stairs to the platform. I got on the train, took a seat, I closed my eyes and said, God, 'as I go to this course, reveal to me my purpose and give me direction in what I am suppose to do in this life'. Friends, this is a prayer that I have prayed time and time again, and before that day, I thought I had found my purpose in life. As I finished praying, it was like a jolt in my spirit and clear as you are reading this book, I heard the words in my spirit and I wrote them down and since that day my life has never been the same again.

What am I saying? Sometimes, we use our life that we lead as a form of rebellion to God, and get carried away with the necessities of this world and forget we are created by the creator for a reason. The things of the world distract us and stop us from achieving our true purpose in life. We end up living an ordinary life and at the end of it all, we are full of regrets of things that were inside us that we wanted to do but never did. If I had spent more time focusing on what was before me, I would not have spent a lot of wasted time chasing after the things I thought were important.

Nevertheless, everything we go through is for a reason, it helps to correct us and guide us as long as we take the lessons learnt from the experiences. And by the way, all the experiences I went through toughened my character and the new skills and knowledge I acquired along the way are and will continually be a benefit to the new direction God is taking me.

So, what is stopping you from walking the path that your creator has laid before you? It is time to take a step out of yourself to find yourself, that is the only way you can make your existence on this earth count.

Preparation Is Key

Before any person embarks on a journey he or she needs to prepare and plan. If you plan to do the twenty five mile marathon, you will have to go through a period of training to build your durability, your muscles and your energy levels. Everyone that has achieved anything of significance has gone through a period of preparation and transformation, lets take two characters from the past and two that are living:

Moses was the original prince of Egypt. A man of good ethics and morals, he loved people. Although did not like unfairness, he was not ready to be the deliverer of God's people until he had gone through his preparation time. I call it the wilderness time or refining time. This is the time, when you build your character, lose all your childish and youthful behaviours, a time to mature and grow your spirit man. It's a time to iron out the good habits from the bad ones, a time of loneliness. Most of the time when you go through your wilderness it is a lonely place. You may have some people around you, however, they are not with you because only you and your creator know where you are. It is normally a time of renewal, it often comes at a time of crisis, when you are at a crossroad in your life; a point when you have to make testing decisions. Everybody has a time of preparation in their life, however, not everybody knows when it comes and will miss the opportunity to develop themselves. Some people end up living a life of missed opportunities. Moses was born for a purpose and God was not going to let him miss his purpose because he was part of the grand plan, even though he altered the timetable a little bit by trying to do things in his own power.

The world would have been a wonderful, so happy place if we all would have just focused on looking for our purpose in life, gone through the training to fulfil the purpose and walked in our purpose. However, we do not have a perfect world and the only person that actually came into this world, fulfilled his purpose to the letter without altering the duration, or the plan was Jesus Christ. Some other religions might contest this fact, however, you cannot contest the truth and if you do, well, there is a day of judgement to think of, and if you contest with that as well, I will leave you to what you believe.

Moses was finally ready at the grand old age of eighty years to fulfil his assignment to deliver the people of God from the hands of Pharaoh of Egypt.

Another man that went through preparation was King David. Before he became king, when he was still a shepherd tending to his flock, he protected the sheep from the bear and the lion. This was the preparation that he went through before he became qualified to take on Goliath, the giant Philistine.

When you are in preparation school, you learn what to say and what not to say, you learn the time to be angry and the time when to be happy. It is a period when you build your value system, your character and attitude. Even Jesus Christ went through a period of preparation before he started his ministry. It was recorded that he started fulltime ministry at the age of thirty years old.

Your creator will not give you a task to do without first preparing you for it. Think about it; If you will not give your five year old, (that's if you have a five year old) a Jaguar XF Saloon car as a birthday present, even if you promised yourself that his ultimate birthday present from you would be the Jaguar XF Saloon car, you will not give your child the car at five years old, because you know he is not ready for it. In that same vein, your creator will not reveal to you your assignment until you are ready for it.

When I was looking for my assignment in life, I went through a period of preparation to iron out a few flaws in my character and attitude. It took me close to seven years to go through my preparation and identify my purpose. I went through knowledge and skill building, I went through spiritual transformation. I identified new areas of strength and some areas which I thought were my area of weakness, were actually areas of strength for me; I was just far away from who I really was meant to be. The place to be when you are in preparation school is in the presence and in the protection of the creator because he will guide you and sustain you throughout that period of training.

Seasons of Preparation

When in preparation school, you go through different stages in your development process. There are various stages of training you need to go through and you will only graduate from one stage to the other after you have passed the test of that stage. This is a period of 'Character Exercise and Building'. This is the development stage in a person's life, the stage when you are straightened out, taken through the fire and come out on the other side. We all go through these stages at some point in our life. It depends on each person when they go through the different stages of preparation. Sometimes we go through the stages at different times and multiple times if the defects keep re-occurring in our character.

Chapter 6

When I was in primary and secondary school, I had to sit examinations to pass out from one class to the other. When I moved to another class, some of my friends that did not make the grade had to repeat the class and were not promoted until they made the pass mark. The same principle applies in the preparation for your assignment; you go through various tests before you are credible to take the next step in your development into what your creator wants you to do.

Here are some Classes of Preparation to Look out For:

- **Class of Mistreatment:** This is a period when you go through different forms of mistreatment such as; verbal, physical, or mental. This class of preparation can be in the form of an employer speaking down on you, it can also be in the form of bullying, abuse of power and exploitation from people above you or even peers. At some point in our lives whether young or old, we have suffered some form of mistreatment and were to some degree helpless and accepted what happened. These kinds of situations build our character. The mistreatment class is focused on building the inner you, your behavioural and habitual traits that form your character, behaviours such as anger and patience.

- Class of Chastening: This is a period of discipline, when you are deprived of certain things you do. Maybe you are a person that spends excessively, you might lose access to certain privileges such as finance and/or opportunities to spend. It could involve sources of income being lost or withdrawn, certain privileges in a place of employment taken away or even losing your job. In young people, this normally comes from parents, when they are trying to instil certain values into their children. With adults, it comes at a time in life when your creator is trying to discipline you. I went through a time of chastening twice in my life, both during the adult stage of my life. I became stronger in character from both experiences and better for it.

- Class of controversy: This class puts you through the test of dealing with controversial issues and getting into and trying to avoid controversy. You need to be able to deal with men in a honourable manner. It is the point where you learn to be diplomatic and respectful of peoples opinions, here an element of patience is key in passing through this class.

- Class of Credibility: This class is where you put your credibility on the line, your integrity is called into question, are you who you say you are? When you go through the class of credibility, your characters integrity is put to the test, this is when your trustworthiness is called into question.
- Class of Frustration: This class is a time of going through disappointing situations, and being frustrated by people. In going through this class, you learn how to deal with rejection and handle the possibility of not making headway in what you set out to do. You learn the ability of perseverance.
- Class of Prejudice: This class is when you go through a period of injustice and unfairness from people around you and associated with you.
- Class of Separation: This is a time when people stay away from you, when you are isolated and all alone.

Your period of preparation aims to prepare you in fulfilling your assignment. In most cases of preparation, you do not actual know that it is a period of preparation until you come out of it. The time you spend preparing for you assignment is absolutely down to how you deal with the stages of preparation you go through.

You Have To Make It An Obsession: The dreams you have are very important and require you to protect them, however, to achieve them you need to be obsessive in executing the plans. You have to harbour what is called a burning desire for accomplishment. For you to achieve anything of significance, you have to have absolute focus on achieving it. When you search for your destiny with the desire of fulfilling it, you are bound to trace your path to your destination.

Keys For Developing A Burning Passion For Your Assignment

1. **Stay Away From All Distractions To Your Assignment:** Your complete focus needs to be on achieving your purpose in life. The easiest thing to do is to allow yourself to be distracted from your journey to finding your purpose for living. For you to find your purpose, you need to be absolutely focused, like a laser guided missile that is targeted at its mark.

2. **Select The Kind of Responsibilities You Accept:** There are some responsibilities that are not related to finding your purpose, these may

vary. However, it is important to establish what is relevant, and what is not, because when you spread yourself too thin, you end up not being able to direct the required commitment in achieving your vision.

3. **Become An Expert About Your Purpose:** For you to achieve your purpose in life; the task that has brought you into existence, you need to be an expert on the subject. If your purpose is to perform brain surgery, you need to be an expert brain surgeon, that means, you need to constantly update your knowledge on the topic of brain surgery, feed your mind about brain surgery, dream about brain surgery, be obsessed with different techniques and know all about brain surgery. A regular upgrade in your knowledge about your purpose will increase your competence and empower you to perform at your peak performance level.

4. **Do Not Talk About Your Purpose With Anyone Who Has No Regard For Your Purpose:** There will be people who will disrespect and speak ill of you and your purpose, you need to steer clear of these kind of people. Avoid meeting or discussing your purpose with them, so they do not sow seeds of limiting belief concerning your purpose into your

mind. If a person does not believe in your purpose, that means they do not believe in you, and if they have influence over you, they can un-intentionally, sow seeds of disbelief and destruction into your mind and spirit without you even knowing it.

5. **Prepare Yourself For Unusual Misfortune:** When you attempt to fulfil your purpose, you are trying to do good and you are working against evil. All evil is from the devil, Satan, and he will try and disrupt your plans by bringing adversity your way. That's when you will experience different kinds of challenges and obstacles and misfortunes. It is important to understand that all this is part of the devil's plan to derail you from fulfilling your purpose.

6. **Disassociate Yourself From Relationships that Despise Your Purpose:** You need to keep away from people who despise and disrespect your purpose in life. If a person does not respect your purpose, they will not help you achieve it or they will not even encourage you to fulfil it.

7. You are the protector of your vision and only you can defend your vision to those that will criticise you.

You need to make a stand for your vision because it is yours and it is all you have to give. The world is waiting for you to locate your vision because people's lives depend on you walking in your purpose and your destiny.

Key Learning Points

1. The guide to finding our purpose is within us and we need to pull it out.
2. There are people that are waiting on us to fulfil our purpose because their lives depend on it.
3. There are rules guiding you to your purpose.

Chapter 7

Your Purpose

'And who knows whether you have not come to the kingdom for such a time as this?' Esther 4:14

The word purpose has been used in so many circles, some call it destiny, while others call it vision. The different terms are all a result of finding something.

Here we are going to break down the elements that form success and what you need to do to attain the status of being successful.

We are looking at Success, Purpose, Vision, and Goals. These are determining factors of achieving what you have been placed on the earth to do.

In the previous chapter, Evita, was successful. At an early age, born into poverty, she found her reason for existence and she began to walk in it. She did that till her death at the age of thirty three. Your success is always dependent on the effect it has on other people; how your life has affected other people in a positive way. It is so incredible to know that successful people work so hard and are never tired, they always have the drive to do more, to achieve more, they feel there is always something they can do to help things become better.

The creativity that you were born with is continually buried as you grow. The way you were brought up, your environment, your belief systems all begin to change and your mind starts to entertain thoughts of fear and doubt. You begin to warm to a 'play it safe' system of beliefs. These systems are learnt as you grow and form your limited belief system, which is located in your subconscious mind.

If you were born into a poverty stricken family life, your decisions will be shaped by the capacity of your pocket. If the idea of 'I will be somebody' comes to your mind, you look at your circumstances and doubt the thought that came to your mind could ever be your reality. So you simply continue living the same way that you have been all along. Going to a dead end job you don't like, collecting a wage that is never enough, going to church if and when you can, growing old and dying with regrets of the things you could of and should of achieved, but never did; all because you allowed your limiting beliefs to get the better of you.

Chapter 7

For you to have any chance of success in life, you need to identify your purpose. Find out the reason that brought about your being, the reason for your conception. To be successful you need to locate the keys to achieving the success that you so crave. If you didn't crave it, the thought of success would not even come to your mind and you would not be reading this book right now. You being successful, is the service you pay for the privilege to come into earth. Likewise your success is answering the call that was placed on your life. Let me tell you how you came into existence; someone had a problem and prayed; the telephone of heaven rang and the creator decided to send you to solve that problem; so, if you have not yet identified your purpose, somebody is still waiting for an answer to their prayer. Think of all the problems that we haven't found solutions to for instance: the cure to different types of sickness, limited breakthroughs in the areas of science and so on. Our obedience in seeking our purpose is what's going to make this world a better place for you and I, it is what is going to give us the answers to all the mysteries of this world.

Do you know how many sperm cells are released for fertilisation during ejaculation? Well let me tell you, wait for it: between forty million and one point two billion sperm cells are released in one ejaculation and out of all that, only one sperm cell fertilises one egg to create one fetus. Isn't it so amazing that out of all those sperm cells, fighting and jostling for position, it was you, the sperm cell that had your coding, your identity, that survived to take the challenged of being born into the world at such a time as this. Do not take your existence lightly, because if you were not necessary, you would not be here.

All that is required for you to function is placed in the cells that determine your make up, your traits, your attitude and character. You need to understand the kind of importance that your creator placed on you. Your inability to locate your purpose, is causing someone to continue to suffer despite their prayers being answered so many years ago!

It has been said that ignorance is not an excuse for failure and one thing to bear in mind is, you are going to be accountable to your creator for not answering your call to duty.

Key #1: Purpose

What is the meaning of purpose?

The dictionary defines it as the reason for which something exists or is done. So if you are created with a purpose in mind, the question is; why are you not doing what you were created for? Or do you think you were placed here just to wake up, have breakfast go to work, have lunch, do a bit more work eat dinner and go to bed? Oh no, your creator had bigger plans for you, you are part of a big jigsaw puzzle and you need to find your position.

Finding your purpose in life will help you in many areas of your life. It will help you to gain enlightenment and a focus in life. It will help you to determine your capabilities and possibilities in achieving certain goals and tasks you set for yourself, such as relationships, business, career and the lives you touch. Finding your purpose will also help you leave a powerful legacy for your children and their children and so on.

So how do I find My purpose?

One of the key drivers of purpose is passion. Whatever you are passionate about gives you an indication of what your purpose is. It is not the complete answer, however it will lead you in the right direction. You need to find that thing that keeps you awake at night, that you love doing so much that you would do it whether you are being paid or not. The kind of passion that is contagious, a passion that keeps the thing always at your forefront. It's a burning desire that eliminates all limitations to do that thing. What are you passionate about? It is in that direction that your purpose lies.

Some of the most successful people on earth are very passionate about what they do. Take an athlete like David Beckham for instance. A football player, former England international player, he came into the world's limelight when he scored a goal from just a bit over the halfway line of the pitch. That was not the first time he had tried that shot, he had practised it over and over again, he perfected the way he took his freekicks and crosses through constant practice and a burning passion to be the best footballer he could be. And he was the best footballer he could be during his playing career which was very successful.

One of the most passionate people I have read about was Dr. Martin Luther King Jr,. He had a passion for non-violent confrontation of segregation in the United States of America during the late 1950s and the 1960s up till his assassination. Dr. King was so consumed with passion for the Negro people to be treated fairly that he went to jail on a number of occasions, his house was bombed while he was at a civil rights meeting and he finally paid the ultimate price with his life. his passion galvanised a nation into civil disobedience to unjust laws, with non-violent protests being held in different parts of America, all because of one mans passion. his passion was contagious; it takes contagious passion for over a million men to march the nations capital for the right thing. It takes a person with audacious passion to lead a group of people in front of attack dogs and police officers with trigger-happy fingers, pointing guns at non-violent protestors who staged a sit-in at a restaurant to stand up for our civil rights. Dr King was and still is an example of a successful man, he walked his path, he lived his vision and attained his purpose. He said it all in the last speech he gave on April 3, 1968 at Memphis, Tennessee; and I quote;

"I don't know what will happen now. We've got some difficult days ahead. But it doesn't matter with me now, because I've been to the mountain top. And I don't mind. Like anybody, I would like to live a long life; longevity has its place. But I'm not concerned about that now. I just want to do God's will.
And He's allowed me to go up to the mountain.
And I've looked over. And I've seen the promised land.
I may not get there with you. But I want you to know tonight that we as a people will get to the promised land.
And I'm happy tonight, I'm not worried about anything.
I'm not fearing any man. Mine eyes have seen
the glory of the coming of the Lord."

April 3, 1968
Memphis, Tennessee

Excerpts from Dr. King's last speech, before he was assassinated on April 4, 1968

If your passion does not consume you to the point where even death does not scare you, you are not yet ready to be successful. Your passion is a major part of your road map to your purpose in life, what are you passionate about?

'There is no easy walk to freedom anywhere, and many of us will have to pass through the valley of the shadow of death again and again before we reach the mountaintop of our desires'.

Nelson Mandela

Nelson Mandela is another successful person, and despite his age, he is still walking in his purpose. Mr Mandela, former South African President, had a determination to see a free South Africa. He gave up his freedom to see that his people were treated equally in their place of birth during the apartheid regime that was ruling South Africa up to 1990 when he was released from prison unconditionally.

Chapter 7

Mr Mandela refused to lower his values for a conditional freedom, he decided; it is full unconditional freedom or nothing. Mandela was of royal blood, yet he was made to be a slave in his own land due to an unjust system of government called apartheid. He was determined that they would be free at any cost, freedom was his aim. He was so determined in his purpose that in his words before he was convicted and sentenced to life imprisonment on June 12, 1964, at the opening of the defence statement at his trial. On April 20, 1964 in Pretoria, Mandela said, and I quote;

"...During my lifetime I have dedicated myself to the struggle of the African people. I have fought against white domination, and I have fought against black domination. I have cherished the ideal of a democratic and free society in which all persons live together in harmony and with equal opportunities. It is an ideal which I hope to live for and to achieve. But if needs be, it is an ideal for which I am prepared to die.'

This statement was made when he was possibly going to be executed. As he was charged with treason, Mandela had the passion and determination even to the point of death. He had resigned himself to his future, he knew his purpose and he was walking in it, up to the point that they charged him to court with the possibility of being executed.

Most people that are successful have a passion for helping people work towards creating a better life for themselves, they are change initiators.

Every generation has it's share of successful people, and their lives have influenced the masses from all walks of life. From sportsmen to world leaders: Mohammed Ali, loved entertaining people, putting a smile on their face, but one thing about Mohammed Ali was, he also had a passion to see black America free of oppression and victimisation. Nelson Mandela, wanted to see peace and harmony amongst the white and black people in South Africa. All successful people have one thing in common, they are passionate about helping people.

There are various ways to identify what you are passionate about, it is normally something you aim to correct, or an act that you hate. It may even be attached to something you love, you need to look inward to seek the answer to identifying your purpose.

Finding Your Purpose

From the previous paragraphs we saw that our passion is closely linked with our purpose, so we are going to track down what our purpose is. Your purpose is unique to you, every man and woman has a unique assignment in life.

Guide #1 What Motivates You

Your purpose is hidden in what motivates you. What gets you going? What are the activities you participate in? You need to be self-motivated to reach your purpose in life. Find that activity that you will do if there is nothing stopping you from doing it, if there are no obstacles or obstructions keeping you from achieving it.

To reach your full potential in life and be successful, you need to identify the activities that drive you. Make a list of the major activities that drive your day. After identifying these activities, you need to identify the different actions you need to take to accomplish these activities or tasks. When you are carrying out this exercise, you should write all the activities down, up to about ten if you can. Also write out the plans or actions you take to achieve these tasks, then analyse the tasks that are rewarding and beneficial to you and to the people around you. Put the list of tasks in an order of priority and keep them close to you, if you can associate passion with any of these tasks, you are moving close to your purpose. These things maybe activities that you have done in the past that you have not been able to do in your present circumstances, that is why it is important for you to set aside time to perform this exercise of finding what motivates you.

Guide #2 What Drives You

Every person has a manual that guides their existence. Political parties have a manifesto, and so do all successful people. The successful go by principles that govern their ideals, what they believe in, and what they stand for. In order for you to be successful and purpose driven, you need to have a manifesto that guides what you do; your own guiding principles. Everything that man has created and manufactured has a manual that tells you how it works and how to get the best out of it. So if you were created in the image of a creator and you have the mind of your creator and have the intelligence to have a manual for whatever you create, how much so the creator of you and I? You have a manual of what makes you who you are, it is your value system. It is what you believe in, it is what you know to be right. Some of us have different beliefs and values that guide us, some are positive and some negative. A negative guiding principle can only lead to destruction and strife. What are the values that guide the decisions you make? What do you stand for? The next step in finding your purpose is to make a list of about ten of your values or guiding principles; the things you believe in and stand for. Write these down in order of priority, select the most important five values that guide your decision making and put them next to your first list of activities.

Guide #3 Who Is Around You

The reason for your existence is to deliver to people. You are suppose to use what is inside you to influence your generation. Who are the group of people you find yourself associating with?

Are they young people?
Are they old people?
Are they men?
Are they women?
Are they the orphans?
Are they the destitute?

The above list is just a guide of different groups of people that are possibly linked to who you are sent to help.

Who do you have a passion to connect with? Some of us are connected to a generation of people, while others are called to a group of people in a generation. Evita had a purpose to support the poor women and children of Argentina; Martin Luther King Jr., had a purpose to lead the black American people out of their darkest hours in history. The generation you find yourself associated with is most likely the generation and group of people you are sent to. Make a list of all the categories of people that come to your mind, put them in order of priority; place this list with the other two lists that you made earlier.

Guide #4 Form Your Purpose

Your purpose is hidden in the lists that you drew up in guides one to three. Now we are going to create the definite purpose for your life.

Step #1 Analyse Your Activities Against Your Values and People

Take the first activity, the most important one, put it through the list of your values and who does it affect in your second list. So for example; if your are a member of a religious organisation and you have a responsibility in that organisation, check how your religious activity and responsibility fits into your value system and in the third list, who does this activity affect in the list of people you are connected to and associate with. Do this exercise for all the activities on your list.

Step #2 Compile A Statement From the Analysis of the Results

The activities, actions, values, and people that you identify to yourself, will make up the statement of your purpose in life. This statement constitutes the manifesto of your life. Now you have created the manual that guides everything you do, and every decision you make. Now you know your end point and the path you are going to take to get there. The next stage of the process is to formulate your plan of action and document it and place it with your manifesto. Now frame your manifesto and its guiding principles.

Step #3 Acquire The Knowledge To Achieve Your Purpose

For you to achieve your purpose in life, you might need further education to be an expert in what you are suppose to do. You might have raw talent, however, talent can only take you so far, if talent could achieve greatness, I am sure all the nations that breed great footballers in Africa should have won the world cup by now. Talent that is not harnessed, developed and focused to a definite end can be lost amongst the crowd. You might move too quickly or even too late, it is important to gain the necessary knowledge to use your talent and guide your passion and determination into effective use.

Lets take a look at tennis players. Despite the fact that some of them possess loads of talent, they still need coaches to guide them to winning the different tournaments they go into.

Step #4 Take The First Step

Now that you have identified your purpose in life, the next stage is to take the necessary steps to work it. You have to take that step that will lead you into living a life of abundance and fulfilment. You are the architect and builder of your castle to success, you are the designer and master craftsman of your future. Now, you can design your future whichever way you like. You can paint that masterpiece that you have been dreaming of. Now that you have documented your success plan; which consists of your purpose; your guiding principles, which is the plan and the action you will take to realise your purpose.

Read your purpose regularly, try a minimum of two times a day. Protect your purpose from those that do not believe in it.

Your manifesto should be guided by deadlines and dates. You also need to state what you will pay for the achievement of your purpose. Count the cost of achieving your destiny, be realistic about it, remember the statement, 'success is not cheap'; many successful people have given their lives, some have given their lifetime. Also remember this statement, 'success doesn't come easy, it takes hard work, commitment and dedication' I am sure I mentioned this earlier.

Finally, call your definite purpose into your conscious mind, let it be all you think about, burn it into your memory. Look for events that connect you with your purpose and attend these events Become one with your purpose and then your purpose will become one with you.

Key Learning Points

1. Your passion will lead you to your purpose.
2. uccess is finding out why you were created and walking the path.
3. Your motivations, your values and the people connected or associated to you make up your purpose.
4. You need to draw up a manifesto of your life that will guide your daily living.

Chapter 8

Success 'Your Destination'

I assume you are wondering, does this really work? Well, let me tell you this, If you think you can or you think you can't, you are right because, you are the builder of your future. The names and people mentioned in this book are a fraction of the successful people walking and living a fulfilled life daily. You do not have to necessarily be rich, however, it is good to be rich. Let me tell you a story I came across one day:

A single mother of five kids in Soweto, known by the name Mama Carol, also known by the name, 'The Angel of Soweto', noticed that many children were being orphaned by aids in her community. In an amazing set of life changing coincidences, she ending up caring for nine hundred and eighty children in child-headed households (these are households where the parents had died as a result of the aids virus). She started an organisation that provides social welfare, food, school fees, school uniforms and any needs that they might have.

In her own words she said, 'I am a 49 year old single mother of five kids, and I trained in hotels. I've been working in hotels for the most of my life until in 1998 when I changed jobs for the fact that the hotel that I was working in closed down. I started training as a nurse, but during my training as a nurse I would do community work. One day the matron came to me and said I had to decide. She said, she understood community work was Ok, but my work as a nurse was more important she said to me, 'make a decision'. There was no way that I could decide between my work and the community. I knew there was going to be no salaries afterwards, but what I did was I just gave up my work and started to work with Sandile's family. Immediately after his mother passed away, that's when I took the story to a local newspaper and had it all published. Before I knew it I was a mother to seventy nine kids, and then it was one hundred and four. Presently we have nine hundred and eighty kids that we're looking after, in two hundred and twelve households.'

When asked how she likes being a mother to nine hundred and eighty kids, she said,

'...fully, I am just so fulfilled, I get so much fulfilment from doing it, fulfilment that I have never... that surpasses all understanding. Fulfilment that I have never ever gotten and from the fact that each and every one of them has a story, there is a story behind them and I try to remember each and every story, each and every incident on how I met them and I keep that in mind so that, like, I can keep them important.'

What is Success?

Success is a never ending journey. Your success can only be measured when you have come to the end of your journey in life, that's when you can look back and see that you have emptied out all you've had to offer your generation. Being successful is accomplishing you purpose in life. Success is subjective to each individual however, all successful people have something in common, they have an understanding of why they are on this earth, they have an understanding of their purpose in life, and they have a focus on the goals of their life. Successful people are those that have discovered their purpose and are walking in it.

First you are born, then you find out the reason why and then you accomplish that reason to improve your generation. Success does not come easy and it does not come cheap, however, success is rewarding. Our life was designed to achieve success, but the world system has programmed your mind to live an average life, just getting by and living on the merry-go-round of life.

Obstacles To A Successful Life

Success achieved through continuing to persevere.

There are reasons that stop people from achieving success in life, obstacles that seem to be impossible to overcome. It is very easy to be unsuccessful, but on the other hand the effort that is required to attain success is harnessed over years of training and preparation. Persistence takes a lot of effort while giving up takes no effort at all. Successful people are persistent in achieving things, they outline a plan to achieve and have a plan B, C and D. Listed below are obstacles to be aware of when navigating your path to success.

1. **If You Lack Desire You Can Never Be Successful.** If you do not have the desire to be successful, there is no way on this earth that you will achieve any form of success. For you to even smell success, you need to have a burning desire to experience success. Success is not going to come

to you if you do not have a hunger for it. A lot of people live on hopes and wishes, but no desire. They want the good things in life, but that is just it, they want them. You need to acquire a burning desire if you want to be successful or else you won't see the success you want.

2. **If You Lack Sense of Worth You Will Never Be Successful.** Having a sense of being unworthy of success is another obstacle to being successful. If you come from a background that is not success oriented, you can build up a mindset of under achieving. Everyone was born with the mindset to achieve, it is hidden deep inside your heart and it will take effort to dig it out. You need to change your attitude towards yourself and believe that you can achieve success for it to happen for you.

3. **If You Fail To Plan You Plan To Fail.** The reason for anything successful is a good plan. No success comes by accident or mistake, it is carefully planned. If you have noticed, we have made emphasis on making lists, writing out strategies and careful planning, it is important to create strategies to achieve your purpose in life. If you do not plan your life, life will plan it for you, and you will live a life

of un-fulfilment. Planning starts by setting goals and targets, as well as outlining strategies in order to achieve your goal.

4. **If You Lack Knowledge and Skills You Will Not Be Successful.** Many people have given up on trying to be successful because they lack the knowledge to achieve what they desire. A lack of knowledge or skill is not the end of the world because, knowledge and skill can be acquired. Knowledge and skill are not the main keys but they are important keys to success.

5. **If You Have Limited Beliefs You Can Not Be Successful.** You need to believe in the impossible for it to be your reality. Having limitations in what you think you can have will put a block on your mind to think of the things you should have. Only you can stop your success through what you do and/or what you think. I am not saying you should be unrealistic in your thinking, what I am saying is, if you want to own a car and no one has owned a car in your family, start by getting a licence. Next, go look at cars, visit car showrooms, sit in a car, believe you can have the car and eventually the car will be yours. Do not think that you are going to have a private jet in a year, when you don't even own a motorcycle.

6. **If You Have Fear In Your Heart You Can Not Be Successful.** Fear is the biggest reason why success eludes a lot of people. There is the fear of so many things such as failure, rejection, death, etc. Fear has haunted so many people and caused multiplied potential success stories not to be realised. Fear is the spirit that will always question your qualifications to be successful. Fear will question your competence. Fear stops you from realising the dreams that are inside you. The only way to combat fear is to believe that you can achieve anything you set your mind to do. Fill your mind with faith and believe in possibilities and your beliefs will become your reality.

7. **If You Lack Discipline And Are Not Willing To Sacrifice You Can Not Be Successful.** If you are not disciplined and are not willing to put in the time, success will most definitely elude you. Success is built over time, the same way your character is built over time. You go through various tests and learn the rules of life, you build a habit of success to be successful. You create time for all the necessities in your life, such as your spiritual growth, your family life, your physical life, your personal life. You live out a balanced life.

8. **If You Do Not Put In The Effort You Can Not Be Successful.** If you are looking for a quick fix to being successful, you are going to be looking for a long time because, there is no shortcut to success. It is a long road, like a marathon, it requires endurance and effort. One of the reasons why people are not successful is because they give up in the middle of the journey even though they were so close.

Every obstacle listed above can be overcome by simply changing your attitude. You are the architect of your life, and the master builder of your destiny. You are the only person that can breakdown the structures of failure in your life and replace them with structures of success.

Keys To Being Successful

There are two main keys to being successful; the first is to find your purpose in life and the second is to walk in your purpose to fulfilment. It sounds simple, however, it takes quite a bit of navigation. The hard part is to finding your purpose; this takes a lot of planning, preparing, searching, trials and errors before you come to the full realisation of your purpose. The initial chapters have taken you through the process of reprogramming your former nature into your new nature of being an individual with a positive mindset and a good attitude. The next stages involve identifying what the meaning of purpose is and how to find your purpose and walk in it.

Seven Character Traits of A Successful Person

You are the main attraction of your life and it is you that will determine the direction your life decides to take. For the benefit of your generation, it will be a great choice to take the successful path that takes you to your destiny. Over the last chapters we have focused on finding who you are in order to take you to where you need to be, but if you do not know when you have reached your destination, you might continue on an unnecessary journey. Knowing the characteristics of a successful person will allow you to stop searching and start walking in your new found purpose.

1. **A successful person is very hard working.** They do not believe in things coming easy, they strive, set targets, and set goals; they are always working. This person does not believe in an easy ride in life.

Success requires hard work and only people who are willing to put in the effort attain it.

2. **A successful person is an honest person.** Integrity is their watchword. Their word is their bond. Their Yes, means Yes and their No, means No. They follow laid down rules, and live by a positive value system.

3. **A successful person always perseveres.** They never give up. A successful person does not let an obstacle keep them from achieving a goal or a task. They do not quit on the job. It is unimaginable the amount of breakthrough ideas that would have gone untold because they never happened? All because someone decided to give up, to quit.

4. **A successful person is friendly and loves people.** You will not find a truly successful person that does not love people. Take all the names we have mentioned in this book, Evita, Nelson Mandela, Martin Luther King, Mohammed Ali, they all loved to serve, educate, encourage and help people. This characteristic enables them to help others and attracts people to them in accomplishing tasks.

5. **A successful person has a teachable spirit.** They are habitual learners, they never stop searching for knowledge. Successful people are always looking for and finding ways to expand their knowledge base. They are constantly searching for new information; learning is their key to breakthrough.
6. **A successful person always goes the extra mile.** They deliver more than is expected of them all the time. The statement that was bouncing around a lot, 'under-promise and over-deliver' was made popular because it created a lot of successful people, including the richest man in the world - Bill Gates.
7. **A successful person is always looking for solutions to problems.** They view problems as opportunities, as stepping stones to solving problems. They do not complain about problems but thrive on them, they always find the solutions.

Your Vision Statement

Before you can get somewhere you need to know that there exists. You need to have a vision of your destination. If you decide to go on holiday to an exotic Island, you would have pictured in your mind what the location looks like, you will get brochures of the area, and information about what to expect, well, the same goes for you. If you are going to live a life of fulfilment, you need to draw up the vision of where your life will be when you get to your destination. A picture of what your life will look like. Your vision is the dream of your fulfilled life, your future destination. It is the story of what you have accomplished with the time you spent on earth. It is all about your future, the American mythologist and philosopher, Joseph Campbell said;

'a dream is your creative vision for your life. A goal is what specifically you intend to make happen. Dreams and goals should be just out of your present reach but not out of sight. Dreams and goals are coming attractions in your life.'

The vision of your life is a picture of where you would be and not where you are; it is your final destination. It is where you see yourself ending up after all has been said and done. It is what will be, or what you want to be said about you at your funeral. The vision of your life is your eulogy.

You attain success when you accomplish your vision in life. Your vision is for you and to you alone, no one can accomplish it for you. Your vision statement gives you focus and allows you to look into the future and make your future. It gives you the opportunity to use all the compositions of your being to deliver to your generation.

Creating Your Vision Statement

The beautiful thing about creating your vision statement is, you get to use your imagination. You also get to tap into your brain power to travel in your mind to your future. The great thing too is, once you get there it is easy for you to work your way back there in the natural because you know where you are going, you have been there before. Here are some steps to creating your vision:

1. Close your eyes and imagine yourself in your future, see yourself as being successful. Everyone's definition of success is different, so make your definition of success particular to you; what you want to achieve, what lives you want to touch, what you will be doing or what you would have done. Once you have reached the pinnacle of your success, in your imagination, hold that thought. Now, burn that thought into your subconscious mind for about five to ten minutes, open your eyes and write what you saw down.

2. The next step is to plan your daily agenda around the vision statement you just wrote down. That means everything you do will be based around your vision statement. You plan your life around the vision statement, these are your guiding principles to your vision statement, they will help you navigate your way.

Your vision ties in with your purpose, your vision enforces your purpose. It leads you in the direction of your purpose.

Guiding Questions for Developing Your Vision Statement

1. hat are your core values?
2. What are the things I enjoy doing the most?
3. How do you spend your time?
4. If you never had to work another day of your life, what would you do with your time?
5. What are your talents?
6. What are your strengths?
7. What are your passions?

8. What is your spiritual, social, physical and financial life like?

9. When lying on your death bed, what would you regret not achieving?

With this armour, you are ready to create your future and make your mark. There have been great vision statements made by extremely successful people, non other than the likes of; Nelson Mandela, Dr. Martin Luther King Jr., President John F. Kennedy, Mother Theresa, Mohammed Ali to name a few; these are people that all left a legacy and some are still leaving their legacies on this earth today by having a vision statement; they worked or are still working towards it's realisation. The decision to become a successful person lies solely with you, the question is whether you will rise to the plate or not.

Epilogue

I know someone was not aware of these principles and guidelines until he came to a crossroad in his life, but when he found them, he decided to take the first step, as he had nothing to loose. Taking that first step was the best decision he ever made. It took him on a journey of realisation through some highs and a few lows, but he came through it and he is living a happy and fulfilled life because he found his purpose in life.

What is your position in life today, are you fulfilled? Are you just getting by living an average life? Do you want to have meaning to the things you do? Well, a connection with what your creator has for you and building a relationship with him is a major step to fulfilment in life. However, to live a maximised life with no regrets and full of abundance, you need to locate your place in the jigsaw of life.

What is that thing, that you have in your hand? What talent or skill do you exhibit that you think is of no use? It might be what your creator put inside you that will guide you to your purpose in life.

David had his sling and five smooth stones, Bill Gates had his computer, Thomas Edison with his hands of inventing, Mother Theresa with her compassionate heart. All these people have visited this planet and achieved their destiny and fulfilled their purpose, but, we have others that have also made their appearance on this planet and fulfilled nothing. They just passed through and were of no benefit.

Today is your day to make a conscious effort to take your place in your generation and fix the part of the world that you have been destined to fix.

The guidelines and principles in this book have been tried and tested. I am a result of following these guidelines. Many of the examples in this book were examples of other people that followed these guidelines. Most if not all successful people have followed these guidelines and have some of the traits discussed in this book.

Our generation is going through an identity crisis, and it is important for us to be reminded of who we are and what we are here to do. Our lives are suppose to count for something. We were placed on this earth to deliver something. Are you going to finish reading this book and make the necessary alterations in your life? Or will you continue doing what you have always done in order to arrive at the same results? I can tell you for a fact, if you change your thinking, you will change your life, it changed mine.

References

1. www.personalitypage.com
2. Wikipedia
3. OHTV
4. The Bible, New King James Version
5. The Message Bible
6. The Science of Personal Achievement by Napoleon Hill
7. Napoleon Hill's Keys to Success: The 17 Principles of Personal Achievement. Edited by Matthew Sartwell

www.ingramcontent.com/pod-product-compliance
Lightning Source LLC
Chambersburg PA
CBHW021104080526
44587CB00010B/381